Copyright © 2002 by Dorothy C. Buck

All rights reserved under International and Pan-American Copyright Convention. No part of this book may be reproduced in any manner whatsoever without written permission except in the case of brief quotations embodied in critical articles and reviews.

Published by Khaniqahi Nimatullahi Publications
U.K.: 41 Chepstow Place, London W2 4TS
U.S.A.: 306 West 11th Street, New York, N.Y. 10014

Library of Congress Cataloging-in-Publication Data

Buck, Dorothy C.
Dialogues with saints and mystics : in the spirit of Louis Massignon /Dorothy C. Buck ; foreword by Herbert Mason.
p. cm.
Includes bibliographical references.
ISBN 0-933546-75-0 (pbk. : alk. paper)
1. Islam--Relations--Catholic Church. 2. Catholic Church--Relations--Islam. 3. Muslim saints. 4. Christian saints. 5.
Saints--Comparative studies. 6. Christian hagiography. 7. Massignon,
Louis, 1883-1962. I. Title.
BP172.5.C3 B84 2002
261.2'7--dc21
2002013642

Printed in the United States of America

Typeset in Caslon
Designed by James Killough

Cover: Detail of "Franciscans Before The Sultan," by Giotto

Dialogues With Saints and Mystics
In the Spirit of Louis Massignon

by Dorothy C. Buck

Khaniqahi Nimatullahi Publications
London, New York

With love to Nicole and Daniel Massignon

Table of Contents

Foreword 13

Introduction 17

1. The Search For Spiritual Truths: Joris Karl Huysmans
   and Saint Lydwine of Schiedam 25

2. The Call of The Divine: Louis Massignon
   and Charles de Foucauld 45

3. Voicing the Inexpressible: Saint Thérèse of Lisieux
   and al-Hallaj 91

4. The Witness of A Saint: Saint Francis
   and The Journey to Islam 113

5. The Feminine Spirit: Mary Kahil
   and the Substitutes 139

6. Two Prayers From The Heart: Christine the Admirable
   and Joan of Arc 167

7. The Eternal Feminine: Mary and the Virgin Heart 185

8. A Sign of Hope: The Mystery of the Legend
   of the Seven Sleepers and the Spiritual Journey 211

Afterword 235

Notes 237

Bibliography 253

Profile 261

Dialogues With Saints and Mystics

In the Spirit of Louis Massignon

Foreword

DOROTHY BUCK HAS WRITTEN her Dialogues "for those who know they are skeptical and materialistic and yet still find themselves wondering about the meaning of life....."

She is a pilgrim herself and her book is an insightful illustration of her personal pilgrimage. Wife, parent, professor and Pastoral Counselor, professional ballerina and teacher of ballet, she is the author of a previous book, The Dance of Life and a beautiful new retelling in blank verse of the Swan Maiden legend included in her doctoral dissertation at Boston University. She is a tertiary Carmelite and someone whose life has been full yet whose spiritual devotions propel her further still. In this instance she is moved by correspondences with other pilgrims, both past and present.

At a certain point along the way, in the mid-1980s, she discovered the late French Islamist and Catholic scholar, Louis Massignon whose many friends and spiritual correspondents became her own. It was through them that she found her own connection to him confirmed and her devotional and ecumenical direction both deepened and enlarged. Her chapters reflect this spiritually intimate relationship, and in doing so they add a dimension to our understanding of the guide and guided experience.

Though she never met Louis Massignon, who died in 1962,

she first came to know him objectively and not, like so many of his contemporaries, as one who had been either overawed or repelled by his erudition, Islamized Christian faith, blend of conservative and radical politics, complex personal history and tendencies, and overwhelming energy and moral scrupulosity. He was to her as to many others, however, bigger than life. It is a tribute to her intelligence and, may I say, feminine instinct that she saw in him an essential simplicity which he admired in others but could never find in himself. Her work, far from being hagiographical or romanticizing of him is sober and at times even starkly honest, despite (or because of) its simplicity of spirit and style. Frankly, she looked beyond him to his guides, whose relics he bore devotedly, and beyond them to the incarnate God whose presence he clarified as being the real center of his as well as of her spiritual life.

Her Dialogues are personal appreciations and affirmations of the value and urgency of pilgrimage. They begin in "search," extend through friendships that overreach centuries of time as witnesses of intimacy, and end with a "legend" found in both Muslim and Christian sources that calls for the ultimate sacrifice and trust of pilgrims.

Readers who "still find themselves wondering about the meaning of life" will be both sensitized and rewarded by this deeply affectionate and serious book, rooted as it is in the practice of faith and totally free of self-posturing. Pilgrimage is illuminated in its pages, especially by her reflections on Louis Massignon's enigmatic yet guiding theme of "substitution" and on her own personal guiding theme of "the virgin heart." It is a work of homage to those who have witnessed both.

Herbert Mason
Phillipston, MA October 2000
University Professor and William Goodwin Aurelio Professor of History and Religious Thought, Boston University

Introduction

I WROTE THIS BOOK for those who know that they are skeptical and materialistic and yet still find themselves wondering about the meaning of life and the possibility that there is a God who calls us into being and invites us to experience life as spiritual. Very often it is the life stories and writings of others that lead us towards discovering our own meaning and direction in life. I believe that we betray our own humanity if we ignore those spiritual seekers who have gone before us, leaving behind their life experience and spiritual wisdom to inspire and guide us. This is a book full of inspiring stories, and lives inspired by their experience of the divine. All of these stories are about people, some of whom were biblical figures, whose lives were radically changed, in a slow growth process over time or in an overwhelming moment of clarity and vision. All of them attributed their transformation to the spirit of God breaking into their lives and leading them to the mystery, without factual evidence or reason, of the way of knowing that we call faith. The life stories in this book were chosen because they were vitally important to the spiritual journey of the French scholar and mystic, Louis Massignon. His is an important voice from the twentieth century whose life was dedicated to religious and inter-cultural dialogue and tolerance. This book is written in the spirit of this man who I have only experienced through his own life story and writings, yet have come to know as a spiritual presence and guide.

I was first introduced to Louis Massignon by Professor Herbert Mason at Boston University. Professor Mason met Massignon in 1958 in Paris when Massignon was 75. The renowned professor from the Collège de France was demonstrating in the streets of Paris for an independent Algeria, meanwhile celebrating Mass every day in Arabic as a Greek Catholic Melkite Priest. He had spent 50 years studying the life and teachings of a tenth century Islamic mystic known as al-Hallaj, and it was that four-volume work that Mason was asked to translate into English after Massignon's death.

In a verse narrative poem on the swan maiden mythology that I was working on I wrote that the swan maiden would never lose her "virgin heart." Professor Mason pointed out to me that Massignon had found this idea in the mystical writings of al-Hallaj. I began to search through Massignon's many books and articles for the sources of the theme which Massignon called *le point vierge*. I began to write articles about it and in the process, like Mason, I found myself drawn into Massignon's world of relationships with saints and mystics. It seems that once Massignon came to know a person or a religious mystic or saint each of them somehow entered deeply into the heart of his own life and remained there from then on, forming a gathering of souls joined to his forever. I call them Massignon's communion of saints.

Louis Massignon and al-Hallaj are not well known in the English-speaking world. Aside from the biographical introductions in Mason's books there is one serious biography in English. That is perhaps as it should be since Massignon himself felt that his life was about revealing to others the witness of those saints and mystics that he so meticulously researched and documented, so that these great mystical lovers could point the way for the rest of us towards their God. It is for this reason that I have chosen to write these stories and reflections.

Louis Massignon was a scholar, a diplomat, an intellectual, and a prolific researcher and writer, yet he was also a mystic.

His struggle to integrate these two apparently discordant sides of himself into his personal and professional life makes him a particularly valuable contemporary spiritual guide. The roots of his spirituality are found in the heart of his relationships to saints and mystics, mentors and friends, as well as to other cultures and religions. Yet Massignon would be the first to insist that all the life stories, quotes and reflections in this book are meant to lead us beyond them and ourselves towards God.

Sometimes a few words spoken or read so affect us that our lives are forever changed. This was true for the young Louis Massignon in 1907 when he read the words of the 10th century Islamic mystic, al-Hallaj, in a book by the Persian poet, Attar. Massignon could not have known in 1907 at the age of 24 that this first irresistible attraction would lead him from undertaking a dissertation on the life and teachings of al-Hallaj to a lifelong relationship that began with his own religious conversion in Baghdad in 1908. In the midst of the Muslim world Massignon had an experience of God breaking into his life, bringing him to his knees to utter the first words of prayer that came to him, surprisingly in Arabic, "God, God! Help my weakness."[1] Drawn inexplicably back to the Catholic Christian tradition of his childhood, Massignon was convinced that it was Hallaj who mysteriously enticed him to Baghdad and that the Muslim mystic was surely one of the intercessors responsible for his unusual conversion experience. This event became a pivotal one that he referred to throughout his life.

Louis Massignon died at 10:45 pm on October 31, 1962 at the age of 79. He had become a renowned Islamist, a man consumed by his passion for learning, for justice and for God. As a professor at the Collège de France he was known for his dynamic lectures. He was a linguist who easily spoke ten languages and read many more. As a world traveler and French diplomat he was a friend to scholars, artists, writers, mystics and popes. His conversion to Christianity in the midst of the Islamic world was the beginning of sixty years of research and association with the Arab culture. He recognized that loving one's neighbor is to "cross over" to others, embracing them as friends, learning to tolerate differences, and in the process finding one's own beliefs, values, and religious convictions enhanced by the experience. In his seventies, his passion for justice led him to demonstrate in the streets of Paris on behalf of his Arab and Muslim friends during the Algerian struggle for independence from French colonialism in the nineteen fifties and sixties.

Always conscious of God's Spirit moving his life, he first answered the call to marriage and family, then in November 1931, after years of reflection on the connection of St. Francis of Assisi to Islam, became a Third Order Franciscan. On January 28, 1950 he was ordained a priest of the Greek Catholic Melkite Rite. Massignon was acutely aware of the tapestry of lives, both living and dead, that intersected with his own. The Islamic mystic Hallaj became not only a subject for scholarship but a spiritual guide whose influence continued to inspire him for a life time. He was drawn to seek out other French Catholic intellectuals, some of whom also had adult experiences of religious conversion. And he was exposed to more and more mystical writings at the suggestion of his mentors and friends.

In the 1880s there was still an aura of Catholic tradition in France with the Saints and mystics seen as witnesses to the Divine Presence in the world. In fact, Massignon was born ten years after Saint Thérèse of Lisieux, the French Carmelite nun who prematurely died at the age of 24 in 1897 leaving us a rich source of spirituality in her writings. Both were born into a climate of colonialism, and social and political insecurity as France struggled to establish the Third Republic and move into the new industrial era. The difference in their families illustrates the issues at stake at the time.

Louis Fernand Jules Massignon was born on July 25, 1883 in a suburb of Paris. His mother was a devout Catholic while his father was an agnostic, an intellectual, a sculptor and engraver, well known in Parisian artistic circles. The young Louis was introduced to both world views and ultimately lived out a portion of both.

Thérèse Martin was born in 1873 in the small French town

of Alençon surrounded by a devout Catholic family and community secure in their faith. The social and political tensions between the intellectual, and largely agnostic, republicans and the traditional Catholic community were felt but caused no internal divisions in her immediate family. Whereas Massignon grew up intellectually stimulated by the artistic, political, and social atmosphere of a big city, Thérèse was sheltered by the cohesiveness of a small town. Yet, both were products of an environment and an era where religion was still a vital force and not easily ignored.

Throughout Massignon's childhood and adolescence his mother provided religious education while his father encouraged his natural intellectual curiosity and artistic sensibilities and assured his education in the best schools. Before trips to other countries his father guided his education in their languages and culture. By the time he was 17 Massignon was moving away from the Church and towards the intellectual atmosphere provided by his father's connections with literary and artistic friends and colleagues. His father's only Christian friend was a novelist named Joris Karl Huysmans to whom he sent his son for a visit on October 27, 1900. Huysmans had written about his own conversion to Catholicism in 1891 in three novels and was in the process of writing a biography of Saint Lydwine of Schiedam at the time of this visit.

Massignon was then sent to Algeria in 1901 and exposed to the desert for the first time. The experience had a profound affect. As he pursued his intellectual interests he found them leading him back to the desert, ultimately throughout his life. Early on in his studies he found a book by the hermit-priest Charles de Foucauld which was helpful in his research of the geography of Morocco. He wrote a letter to Foucauld which eventually led to a relationship that influenced him and continued to intersect with his life well beyond Foucauld's untimely death in 1916.

Massignon was a passionate person who was intensely drawn to the spirit in other people and sometimes his enthusiasm spilled over into physical attraction. He was deeply affected by the suffering of others and particularly sensitive when he felt that he was responsible for another's pain. He had a deep affection and affinity for women starting with his relationship with his own mother. His friendship with an Egyptian woman named Mary Kahil inspired a profound integration and deepening of his spiritual vocation. Their relationship was truly an example of shared mystical love. This respect for the feminine in his life led him to seek spiritual guidance at well known shrines such as those dedicated to the Virgin Mary and to Saint Joan of Arc. He prayed to other less known saints such as Christine l'Admirable and Anne Catherine Emmerich, and sought out obscure tombs of Muslim saints as well.

He was attracted to the legends and popular devotions that grounded religious traditions in diverse cultures, and sought out their roots. Following the path of evangelization from the East to Europe led him to the discovery of a chapel in Brittany, France dedicated to the Seven Sleepers, a story he knew well from the Koran about seven Christian martyrs. Always seeking to find the bridges to Christian/Muslim relations, he established an annual shared pilgrimage that survives to this day. Massignon experienced the Christian and Muslim saints who he studied and the men and women who mentored and shared his spiritual journey as intercessors who remained connected to him throughout his life. Even Biblical figures such as Abraham became a part of his own spiritual identity leading him to work towards and pray for a reconciliation of all three Abrahamic religions of Jews, Christians and Muslims.

It was these relationships that formed the roots of Massignon's spirituality. He lived a profound experience of the communion of saints, a sense of ongoing relationship with the souls of both the living and the dead. The subject of this book is the life stories and writings, in dialogue with one another, of those spiritual friends, saints and mystics, who influenced and guided him on his unique spiritual path. Inevitably, Louis Massignon himself became a spiritual guide for others encouraging us to discover our own communion of saints as we journey together to fullness of life in God.

Chapter One

The Search For Spiritual Truths
Joris Karl Huysmans and Saint Lydwine of Schiedam

ON OCTOBER 27, 1900, Louis Massignon arrived in the small French town of Ligugé with a letter from his father introducing him to the well-known writer, J.-K. Huysmans. He did not know that the novelist would one day become an important person in his own life. At seventeen years old, Massignon was just finishing High School. This was one more introduction to one of his father's artistic friends; one more effort to expose him to the intellectual and artistic circles that created French cultural life in Paris at the turn of the last century. Massignon's father, Pierre Roche, was a sculptor and Huysmans was unique among his artistic and literary friends because he was a professed Christian. His conversion experience to Catholicism in 1891 was the subject of three of his novels. The young Massignon spent six hours with Huysmans and presumably heard all about the novelist's conversion experience and most likely about his current work on the life of an obscure Dutch saint, Saint Lydwine of Schiedam.

Part One: Joris Karl Huysmans

J.-K. Huysmans was born in Paris on February 5, 1848 into an artistic family, many of whom were painters. His mother was French and his father was Dutch, becoming a naturalized

French citizen after the birth of his son. They named their child, Charles Marie George but later in his life, as a writer, he reclaimed his Dutch heritage, changing his name to Joris Karl. Near the end of his life his interest in Saint Lydwine was another way he reclaimed his Dutch roots.

Huysmans became one of the most renowned and controversial writers of his time. He was an art critic as well as a novelist who prided himself on breaking new ground with every publication. He first accomplished this with his novel *A Rebours* which was published in 1884 and established him as the founder of a new literary movement. Influenced by the "naturalists" associated with Emile Zola, he moved beyond them, expressing the truth of humanity as he not only observed, but as he experienced it himself. His own life was the subject of his novels and the characters were modeled for him by those around him. To read Huysmans' novels is to enter into the author's own passionate struggle with life as he plumbed the depth of his own humanity and that of others in his search for psychological and spiritual truths. At the end of thirty years his novels completed the autobiography of a man who agonized over the plight of human beings seemingly born to temptations of every dimension and brought to despair through physical, mental and spiritual suffering. His biographer writes: "Huysmans could feel justified in stating, as he lay on his deathbed, 'No one has put more of himself into his books than I...'"[1]

Like most French children of the time, Huysmans was baptized a Christian as an infant. He was given the name Charles Marie Georges at the parish of Saint Séverin on the left bank in Paris. Much later this church would again become prominent in his life. As a child he learned some simple Dutch prayers from his grandmother and he would be taken to visit the convents of various relatives whose vocations were to the religious life. Soon however family events would create an unhappy childhood leading the adult artist to search for the meaning of human suffering throughout his life. His father died when he was eight years old and his mother remarried within the year to a Protestant businessman. His mother clearly favored the two girls born of that second marriage. School was no refuge for him either. He was small, and apparently sickly, and painfully suffered the torments of the school bullies. His poverty condemned him in High School as well, where the rich middle class students rejected him. Although he never spoke of his parents in his writings, his experience of school was described in detail by one of the characters in a later novel.[2]

Huysmans went on to work as a Civil Servant while attempting to go to law school but soon discovered he preferred the Bohemian night life of the Latin Quarter cafés. What greater stimulant for the young literary talent than to ardently discuss great poets and writers into the early morning hours? He surrounded himself with a circle of friends, eccentric and marginalized, yet some would become the most well-known artists and writers of late 19th century France. He continued to support his writing as a Civil Servant until he retired. Despite his attraction to the Bohemian life, taking a mistress, and bursting onto the literary scene as a controversial figure, he was not relieved of his impotence, his fear of women and marriage as a road to "frustration and poverty", nor of his conviction that in life "one can expect nothing but the worst."[3]

Huysmans pessimistic view of life and the human condition based on his own painful experiences as a young person caused him to imagine that "suffering was a sign of superiority." In 1882 he had no tolerance for religion condemning the clergy as "intolerant" and believers as "feebleminded."[4] Not only was his own struggle with life and spirituality reflected in the struggle of the heroes in his novels, but they also battled with the major issues of his time, what his biographer calls, "the gods of the 19th century—science and progress, pessimism, and the search for the 'natural' as opposed to the supernatural of past eras of religious conviction."[5]

His first novels voice his boredom and disappointment with life's monotony and apparent futility, yet even in *A Rebours* he leaves us with his own spiritual hunger hanging on the final words of his protagonist who cries out to God for comfort. Ironically his fascination with the occult and the satanic became a bridge to authentic religious experience because it led him to encounter the supernatural and the mystical. It was through the strange Abbé Boullan, whose experiments with the occult and satanic rituals led to criminal offenses and even imprisonment before they met, that Huysmans was first introduced to the mystical idea of substitution, or suffering for the sake of others.

In 1888 in the museum at Cassel in Germany he discovered a painting, the *Crucifixion* by Grünewald. In it he perceived an answer to his artistic search for a way to write that reflected his vision that, "Art only becomes interesting when the senses cease to help us."[6] He called his new approach to the dichotomy of body and soul, matter and spirit, "spiritual naturalism." Thus he wrote in an essay, "to be truly great, a work of art must be either satanic or mystic, for between these two extremes there is only a temperate zone, an artistic purgatory, filled with more or less contemptible works of purely human interest."[7]

In the process of writing a series of essays on the old neighborhoods of Paris in 1890, Huysmans returned to Saint Sèverin and the other churches on the left bank in Paris where he experienced the liturgies, choirs and religious rituals that were to inspire his continuing search for his own soul. Thus in his next novel, *Là Bas*, he expressed an experience of life entirely devoid of God in all of its "immorality, cynicism and depravity"[8] and then, in the voice of his main character, expressed his longing to escape from the chains of his own sensuality and lose himself in a spiritual realm. He desperately wanted to believe. He began to view Christian art and mysticism as his road to inner peace and salvation.

This was not an easy path for Huysmans who, even with his resolve to make a complete change in his life and return to the church, found himself, disappointed in his mistress, seeking solace in a Paris brothel. Heartsick and ashamed he sought out a spiritual director named Abbé Mugnier.[9] After two years of struggle he wrote the Abbé, "You who have always had the faith, if only you knew what it costs to recover it! But I'm so weary, so utterly disgusted with my life that it's surely impossible for God not to have pity on me!"[10] In July 1892, Huysmans travelled to the Trappist Monastery, Notre Dame d'Igny, with the intention of making his confession and First Communion. The night before his scheduled confession was painful and frightening. He suffered erotic nightmares, awakening in terror, sure that he was being visited by Satan. Finally he got up in desperation and went to the chapel. There he found the monks spread out on the floor of the chapel in various postures of intense prayer. Struck by the "figure of an 80 year old monk kneeling before a side altar in an ecstasy of adoration, his coarse and weather-beaten features utterly transformed and illuminated by an inner spiritual radiance—he sank to his knees, humbly begging God to forgive him for soiling this holy place with his presence..."[11]

In his stay at the monastery Huysmans immersed himself in the daily prayers of the monks and found himself slowly transformed. He did receive his First Communion only to find himself confronted with feelings of unworthiness. Awakening to his own spiritual poverty opened the way to the depth of prayer that would change his view of life. The natural world took on a beauty he had not noticed before. Leaving the monastery was painful because he now felt condemned to the life of frustration that he described so poignantly in his novel *En Route*, "still too much of the man of letters to make a monk, and already too much the monk to remain among men of letters."[12] For much of the rest of his life he struggled to find a balance between the two, dreaming of a community of artists who would take up the religious life as Oblates living a communal life outside the walls of a nearby monastery.

Huysmans was constantly reminded of his life-long search for an answer to human suffering. From his childhood he suffered from physical illnesses. As an adult bouts of digestive disorders and rheumatism plagued him, along with his mental battles with the doubts, fears and scrupulosity that profoundly affected his relationships. He watched his former mistress, Anna

Meunier, regress further and further into an incurable mental illness as well as the premature death of his talented young friend, the religious artist, Charles-Marie Dulac. He had hoped that Dulac would join him as a Benedictine Oblate at Maison Notre Dame, his home in Ligugé built near the abbey of Saint Martin. Until now, suffering had seemed to Huysmans only useful insofar as it stimulated artistic creativity. But he was influenced by the preaching of the ex-priest Joseph Boullan on suffering in relation to mystical substitution and by the writings of his former friend, Léon Bloy.

He began to see suffering as a gift from God and a way of reparation for the sins of humanity. Those living monastic vocations dedicated their lives to taking on the world's suffering in order to protect the rest of sin-ridden humanity from the wrath of God. It occurred to him that fewer and fewer were called to monastic life and therefore suffering was a necessary experience for everyone. He wrote, "Without suffering, human nature would be too ignoble, for it alone can uplift and purify the soul."[13]

Yet Huysmans was still unable to imagine willingly suffering himself, and writes admiringly of a young woman who visits him on her way to entering a monastery. "Only once in my life have I seen radiant beauty, divine beauty, the only true beauty. It was in the face of a very plain woman who came to see me one evening. ...In the short time she spent with me she spoke to me of the joys of sacrifice and the delights of suffering—and this plain woman's face was transfigured. Her eyes took on an extraordinary, indefinable expression—but how can one possibly render anything like that? True beauty doesn't lie in form or feature, for these are transformed by a sudden surge of the spirit; religion ennobles everything..."[14] Thus in *La Cathédrale* he documents the path of his own conversion with his increasing devotion to the Mother of God, and his inability, as yet, to accept spiritual and physical pain without complaint, in silent and complete trust in God.

Once again his novel became a focus of controversy, for many could not accept that the author of *A Rebours* and *Là Bas* could experience a true religious conversion. There was even a complaint to Rome. Despite his fame he was tortured by the isolation and loneliness of his life at age 50, writing in his diary on June 20, 1898, "No nothing has gone right, nothing. If I don't enter a monastery I shall have failed in everything: a bachelor life without a woman, marriage, and the cloister."[15]

One final effort to decide whether to enter a monastery led him to a vocation as a Benedictine Oblate and the fulfillment of a dream, to build his Maison Notre Dame in Ligugé. It was there that he wrote his book on Saint Lydwine of Schiedam, "In order to throw a little light, however uncertain, upon the dark and terrifying mystery of suffering," he wrote to a sick woman in a letter dated March 13, 1900.[16] He did not know how much his own suffering at the end of his life would resemble that of the 15th century Saint Lydwine.

In October of the same year the young Louis Massignon visited the 52 year old author. Massignon's father, Pierre Roche, was introduced to Huysmans by the painter, Charles-Marie Dulac and it was Roche, along with Henry Cochin, who organized an exhibit to honor the young religious painter's work after his untimely death. Huysmans was invited to write a preface for the catalogue.[17] What would the intellectually astute and precocious 17 year old Massignon think of the theme of mystical substitution and suffering that was so central to Huysmans' biography of Saint Lydwine? A professed agnostic and eight years away from his own religious conversion, he had no idea that this theme would one day become the cornerstone of his own Catholic faith, made explicit through his life-long exploration of the life of the Islamic mystic and martyr, al-Hallaj. It was only when his father wrote to him that Huysmans had prayed for him on his deathbed in 1907, that he began to recognize Huysmans' significance as an intercessor in his life. In fact, Massignon would discover that Huysmans' influence, along with many others, continued to affect him throughout his life. He named these correspondences, "intersigns". Years after his visit to Ligugé he remembered the symbols of mystical substitution and suffering that surrounded the author in his room at Maison Notre Dame: a reproduction of Grünewald's *Crucifixion*, a simple crucifix, and a photo of a portrait of Saint Anne Catherine Emmerich showing the wound in her hand like those of the crucified Christ, called the stigmata, and the bandage of an ecstatic on her brow.[18]

Perhaps Massignon heard the story of Saint Lydwine during his only visit with the famous novelist. Huysmans may even have explained his views on substitutionary suffering in much the same way as he wrote to the sick woman who wrote to him for consolation. "... Everyone is responsible to a certain extent for the sins of others, and must to a certain extent expiate them; and everyone can also attribute the virtues he possesses or acquires to those who possess none or can acquire none. God was the first to submit to these laws when he applied them to himself in the person of his Son.... He wished Jesus to give the first example of mystical substitution—the substitution of one who owes nothing for one who owes everything—and Jesus in turn wishes certain souls to accept the legacy of his sacrifice and, in the words of Saint Paul, to complete what is lacking in his Passion... if he wishes to continue suffering here on earth, he can do this only in the members of his mystical body.... Unfortunately there are now fewer saints, and the contemplative orders are dwindling in numbers or becoming less austere, so that Our Lord is obliged to turn to us, who are not saints....

Lydwine was one of God's chosen expiatory victims, but it took her a long time to realize this. She suffered physical agonies such as may never be suffered again, simply because she did not wish to suffer. From the day that understanding dawned upon her, she lived in that strange condition in which pain is a source of joy... One should take no account of the spiritual aridity or lethargy, or the impossibility of praying properly, which one experiences when suffering. One should simply offer up one's continuation of the Passion to God. That is all that I know, and all that I can write in Saint Lydwine about suffering. It seems to me to be the truth, and what is more, a consoling truth, for one is never nearer to God, and never more accessible to his influence, than when one is in pain."[19]

Part Two: Saint Lydwine

Lydwine was the only daughter in a family of nine children. She was born on Palm Sunday in 1380, in the small town of Schiedam not far from the Hague in Holland. During her lifetime her world was inundated with the devastation, poverty, and confusion caused by the civil wars and plagues that raged throughout all of Europe. In Holland, feuds among the royalty divided the monarchy, led to uprisings, violent murders, and the destruction and pillaging of whole villages. The Church too was besieged by the corruption of ambitious popes led astray by the lure of money and power and the great schism that ultimately separated the Eastern Churches from Rome. Adding to the confusion was the election of two popes simultaneously, one housed in Rome and the other in Avignon. Disillusionment, overwhelming poverty, and the cruelty of one epidemic after another led to heresies and defiance of the Church through magic, black masses, and satanic rituals. Famine, terror, and disease left common people of faith fatigued and vulnerable.

Into this chaos a litany of great saints appeared and strove to compel reconciliation and restore stability to the Church and their countries. It is this roster of women, born one after another, that inspired Huysmans to envision them as chosen by God to be witnesses to the saving power of suffering. Perhaps the most familiar to us is Joan of Arc, who was put to death two years before Lydwine died, and known as the heroine who restored France to unity. Lydwine too was said to have protected Schiedam and Holland from devastating invasions. She, however, never left her home.

According to the biographies that served as references for Huysmans, Lydwine was a beautiful child born into a poor family and given a name that would one day symbolize the story of her life. Lydwine comes from a Flemish word that means "to suffer" or "great patience".[20] Her childhood was spent helping her mother with the chores of their large family. Very early in her life she took pleasure in stopping to pray in the local church before the statue of the Virgin Mary. As a young girl she was unusual in that she enjoyed solitude more than playing with her many friends. Soon Lydwine was noticed by the young men for her beauty and many wanted to marry her. But Lydwine refused. She wanted to belong solely to God and prayed to become ugly in order to avoid the attention of her young suitors. She had no way of knowing how literally her prayer would be answered.

Lydwine's trials began at the age of 15 when an unknown illness left her very pale and thin. Shortly afterwards her friends invited her to go ice skating with them. When another skater crashed into her, she fell hard on the ice, breaking one of her ribs. The wound never healed, turning into a hard and painful abscess. This was the beginning of her torturous suffering which was to last for thirty-eight years. It was also the beginning of the miracle, for Lydwine lived through the ugly wounds of the black plague, for which there was no known treatment, and every disease that ravaged Europe at the time. No doctor could help her. At first she thought she was condemned by God and didn't understand why she had to suffer while her friends played happily in the streets. She became despondent and hardly prayed at all. The dark night of the soul that Saint John of the Cross describes as a stage in the spiritual journey toward God seemed to overtake her. Huysmans writes, "God plunged her understanding into darkness, her will into indifference, her memory into emptiness, and her heart into bitterness."[21]

After four years with no consolation, a priest named Jan Pot came to visit Lydwine and became her confessor and spiritual guide. He explained that her suffering was a vocation that allowed Jesus to continue to heal the sin of the world through the members of his church, his mystical body. He told her, "The secret of your distress is that you suffer because you do not wish to suffer. Offer your despair and suffering to God and He will lighten it."[22] After a great spiritual struggle Lydwine discovered her own desire to suffer for the souls of others. She would take the road to calvary with Jesus. Like the painful biblical story of Job, Lydwine's faith endured until she found the joy that could sustain her through every torture because she discovered God's hand in it, and knew God's love without doubt.

Lydwine was bedridden for most of her life but soon became known for her spiritual insights. She was visited by hundreds of people seeking healing or advice. Angels were said to visit and console her. Huysmans calls the stories of her mystical visions and journeys with angels, "wanderings of the spirit." Her body was wracked by open sores which never healed and her eyes became intolerably sensitive to light. She lived in extreme poverty yet she gave away all that was brought to her to feed the poor. Lydwine welcomed all who came equally, and willingly helped clergy, royalty, and the very wealthy as well as lowly peasants. She addressed their faults and listened to their fears seeming to be able to read their souls. Some said she knew when something was being hidden from her and even knew what it was.

Meanwhile, Lydwine herself seemed to pass through stages of the spiritual journey experiencing months of dryness in prayer only to be consoled by states of ecstasy. Her fevers came and went and she became blind in one eye, with never-ending pain. Huysmans gives a graphic and detailed description of physical afflictions that no human being could endure much less survive, which seemed clear evidence of their divine origin. Her body became grotesque with open wounds and her facial features distorted beyond recognition yet her bedroom had a sweet scent of perfume rather than the putrid odors of her sickness. Lydwine willingly took on the sufferings of others to relieve them. Her vocation as healer of bodily wounds was unusual in that the wounds she healed became her own. Her prayers were known to effect cures and stay the flames that threatened to destroy the town of Schiedam three times in her lifetime. She was consumed with compassion for others and love for her God, telling her confessor of visions revealing the infinite joys of heaven that encouraged her patient acceptance. Year after year her passion for suffering increased along with her generosity towards others, most of whom were strangers.

In 1433, at the age of 53, Lydwine died and was buried in the graveyard of the Church of Saint John the Baptist. A year later a chapel was built over her tomb. At her request her small house was made into a hospital and refuge for the poor. In 1448 three miracles were attributed to her and on March 18, 1890 she was canonized by the Roman Catholic Church as a Saint. When Huysmans visited Schiedam in 1897 he found the relics of Saint Lydwine contained in a chapel in the church called the Visitation of Our Lady. Her tombstone was preserved in a small Dominican chapel when the church where she was buried was converted to Protestant during the Reformation. There were no portraits or photographs to capture the essence of Lydwine's beauty or her pain, and the wood engravings, and statues or episodes of her life in glass in the churches of Schiedam at the time of Huysmans' visit felt inadequate to him. He did discover that Saint Lydwine had become the patroness of the town.

He writes that Lydwine's story is not unusual or new in the biographies of saints who lived before or after her. Many were said to live without nourishment other than the Eucharist, or without sleep. Some, like Lydwine had wounds which gave off an odor of perfume and there were others where the sweet scent of flowers was noticed after their deaths. Like Saint Francis of Assisi, Saint Anthony of Padua and Saint Catherine of Sienna, Lydwine's body was returned to youth and beauty after she died.

Although Huysmans' intention when he wrote Lydwine's story was to show how her life was an example of mystical substitution, her struggle to understand and accept human suffering was very much his own. In May 1900 Huysmans was unaware that the toothaches and pain in his jaw that he experienced were early signs of cancer.

Shortly after the publication of Saint Lydwine, on March 21, 1901, Huysmans made his solemn profession as a Benedictine Oblate. He took the name brother John after a Benedictine Abbot who shared his love of plain chant and art.

Unfortunately, the abbey of Saint Martin was forced to close. After only two and a half years in Ligugé at his beloved Maison Notre Dame, Huysmans moved back to Paris. He began his work on his final novel, *L'Oblate*, shortly after Lydwine's story was published.

In this novel Huysmans finally answers his question about human suffering by personifying her as the bride of Christ. He envisions Christ as the first in the long line of mystical substitutes who have followed in the spiritual and physical Way of the Cross, like Lydwine. Huysmans' hero finally finds inner peace and acceptance of God's will by stating, "There is so much to atone for. If the divine rod is ready to chastise us, let us bare our backs for it; let us show at least a little willingness…"[23] Huysmans himself was now ready to begin his own Way of the Cross as the painful and increasingly disfiguring cancer in his jaw slowly led to his own death.

He went through torturous visits to the dentist, difficulty eating, and continuous pain. Yet he spent much of his time patiently writing letters of encouragement to those who wrote to him. In 1906 he was taken to a nursing home after having undergone surgery for a tumor in his neck and then the extraction of the rest of his teeth. He returned home. Like Lydwine, he too lost his sight in one eye. As he became increasingly weaker his closest friends came to visit, remarking how patiently he endured the painful redressing of his wounds after surgery and never voiced a complaint. In his last letter to his friend Léon Leclaire he wrote, "My life drags on with influenza added to the rest. I'm not sleeping or eating, but just manufacturing abscesses to the accompaniment of never-ending toothache. Anyone who hadn't the faith and a ha'porth of courage would have blown his brains out long ago. Well, I am not unhappy. The day I said *fiat* [Let it be done according to your word] God gave me incredible strength of will and wonderful peace of mind. I am not unhappy. I do not wish to be cured, but to continue to be purified so that Our Lady may take me above. My dream would be for God to take me with Him like the good thief at Easter, but alas, I am unworthy of that."[24] When a friend visited him for the last time the day before he died, Huysmans whispered, "I am going to God, my dear friend, and I am praying for you."[25]

Huysmans died on Sunday, May 12, 1907 at 7:30 pm. Before his burial, when the coffin was closed, the Abbé Fontaine said, "Lord, you gave him great talent, and he used it for your glory. You gave him great suffering, and he used it for your blessing."[26]

Part Three: The Balance

Huysmans envisions a law of equilibrium, a balance of good and evil, that he calls mysterious. He writes:

> "All through the ages there have been found saints willing to pay, by their sufferings, the ransom for the sins and faults of others, and even now this generosity is hard to understand. Besides our own nature which shrinks from all suffering, there is also the Evil One who intervenes to frustrate the sacrifice... Like the needle of a compass, when it inclines too much to the side of Evil ... God allows epidemics to be unchained, earthquakes, famines, and wars; but His mercy is such that He then excites the devotion of His saints... that his wrath may be appeased and equilibrium re-established."[27]

Huysmans speaks in a language that is foreign to the majority of us who live a fast-paced life in a world careening into the 21st century, even to those of us who profess religious affiliations and values. We have all but lost the concept of words like "evil" and "sin". Perhaps our fear of those ancient religious realities is an avoidance of responsibility. It is painful to admit that there are forces within us that are in conflict. Good and evil feel more like opposing forces in a world of temptations outside of ourselves. But the reality is that they also wage an internal war that is part of the human condition.

Our technology has brought the scenes of Huysmans "evil" right into our living rooms. Not only the atrocities of worldwide genocides, terrorist attacks, and civil wars, but hate crimes against people of different races, religions, and sexual orientations. Where is the balance when the "third world" is steeped in illiteracy, poverty, and disease while the "developed world" indulges its high standard of living, coveting money and more and more possessions? Is there a way of reparation and atonement? Two more ancient religious terms that remind us that we may well have some responsibility in restoring Huysmans' balance of good and evil.

Once there were holy people like Saint Lydwine of Schiedam who answered a call to sacrifice their lives, as Christ did, for the sake of others. Some entered a monastic community accepting a severe way of life, giving up personal possessions and consciously dedicating hours to prayer, penance, and work in the belief that prayers are answered, healing is possible, and a loving God is concerned for all of human life. Today it seems that few are called to the monasteries, and fewer still are called like Saint Lydwine to bear pain and suffering because their souls are strong and their love for God and all of humanity is immense. Thus, Huysmans suggests that because there are so few, God turns to those of us who are not saints to learn to experience our suffering as a mysterious offering of ourselves for the sake of others. He asks,

> "How many of us who are afflicted with chronic or incurable illnesses realize that we accomplish the admirable work of reparation both for ourselves and others?"[28]

It appears to me that the joy in suffering that he describes can only be realized when we accept our own trials and willingly offer them to God. That is certainly easier said than done as Lydwine's story suggests. But by struggling with our own tears and distress we discover compassion for others and finally learn to truly love. God's love lives at the center of every painful experience waiting to be made into our own.

Huysmans knew that he was writing to those of us who know pain and chronic illness well, as he did. He also knew that our need to imagine God as Goodness and Benevolent Kindness does not allow us to find any meaning in our pain and suffering. We need to find God in it or we will struggle in vain against it, creating more pain, as even Lydwine did for some years. Only when I can embrace the beautiful image of Suffering as the Bride of Christ and identify her in my life, as Saint Lydwine did, will my suffering transform into joy.

Suffering: The Bride of Christ

Huysmans' emotionally powerful personification of Suffering as the Bride of Christ begins with Jesus' agony in the garden of Gethsemane the night before his trial and crucifixion. The Gospel according to Luke tells us that "In his anguish he prayed with all the greater intensity, and his sweat became like drops of blood falling to the ground."[29] Huysmans personifies Suffering as a woman and calls Jesus the bridegroom. He writes:

> "Suffering crowned her bridegroom with a sweat of rubies, a diadem of bloody pearls… Suffering accompanied him to the judgement hall, before Herod and before Pilate; she inspected the lashes of the whips; she increased the weight of the hammers; she made certain that the thorns were spiky, that the vinegar was bitter, that the spear and the nails were sharp. And when the supreme moment of the marriage had come, while Mary, Magdalen, and Saint John stood in tears at the foot of the Cross, She, like that Poverty of whom Saint Francis spoke, climbed resolutely on to the gibbet-bed, and from the union of these two outcasts of the world, the Church was born, coming forth in a torrent of blood and water from the victim's heart. And then it was over. Christ had given up the ghost and escaped forever from Her embrace. She had been

widowed in the moment that She had been loved, but She came down from Calvary rehabilitated by that love, redeemed by that death.

Spurned like the Messiah, She had been uplifted with him, and from the height of the Cross, She too had dominated the world; Her mission was now ratified and ennobled; henceforth She was comprehensible to Christians, and until the end of time She would be loved by souls who would call upon Her to hasten the expiation of their sins and those of others, and would love Her in remembrance and in imitation of the Passion of Christ."[30]

Huysmans writes, "Lydwine would assure us that the certain antidote to suffering is love."[31] Taking his cues from her ancient biographers, Thomas à Kempis and Gerlac, he gives us her words.

When she took on the illnesses and pain of others her friends said she would kill herself for people who do not deserve it, she responded:

> "Such is the astonishing ingratitude of human nature that in happiness God does not count. If all the sheep were both fortunate and well, the sheepfold would be empty. It is in their own interest then that the Shepherd should bring them back, and there is no other way than to dispatch after them his terrible watchdogs, sickness and misfortune."[32]

To Priests and those she perceived as knowledgeable in the way of the Lord she would say:

> "If pain is not an exact synonym of love, it is in all cases the means and the sign of it. The sole proof of affection one can give to anyone is to suffer, when possible, in his place, for caresses are easy and prove nothing:…The one who loves the Lord should therefore

wish to suffer for God."[33]

Saint Lydwine reassured those whose pain and suffering left them unable to pray or feel love:

"You are miserable when you do not feel love already flowing in you, but indeed, to weep because you do not love is to love already."[34]

It took the young Louis Massignon many years to discover Joris Karl Huysmans as one of his own spiritual intercessors. His one visit to Ligugé was a seed that planted some ideas and thoughts that did not begin to mature until that fateful time in May 1908 when he had his own radical experience of God. He was in Baghdad in search of sources for the life story of an obscure mystic and martyr of Islam, known as al-Hallaj. For the remainder of his life he referred back to that moment when God broke into his life as the beginning of a life-long conversion experience. It ultimately led him to become a pioneer in valuing and promoting interreligious dialogue, hospitality and compassionate acceptance of others, regardless of differences in culture and religion.

He found an example of Huysmans' mystical substitution in the teachings and martyrdom of the tenth century al-Hallaj who he also experienced as an unusual intercessor in his conversion back to Catholic Christianity. Huysmans remained present to Massignon as a guide and protector throughout his life. He saw an introduction to Huysmans last confessor, Père Daniel Fontaine, as an "intersign" pointing out direction in his life. He confided in Fontaine to help him decide whether to marry or seek out a religious vocation. On January 18, 1922, while working on the sculpture of a bust of J.-K. Huysmans, Massignon's father, Pierre Roche, died in his studio. Massignon found him lying before his "unfinished memorial" to his friend.[35] Louis Massignon understood this event as an invitation to offer himself in prayer for his agnostic father's salvation just as Huysmans, on his deathbed, had prayed for him in 1907, a year before Massignon's own conversion.

Chapter Two

The Call of The Divine
Louis Massignon and Charles de Foucauld

DEEPLY EMBEDDED IN the stories of saints and mystics is a period of time, or a stage in the spiritual quest, that is often described as a "desert experience." Sometimes it feels like a vast interior open space, arid, empty, seemingly devoid of life; an inner wasteland or wilderness. Those who lived in biblical times were concretely familiar with the desert. The first nomadic tribes of Israel physically knew the feel of sand and sun, as did the later Christians and Muslims who shared a common heritage through the great patriarch, Abraham and those same twelve tribes that once made up the nation of Israel. These religious ancestors of ours knew the hidden oasis of life teeming beneath the barren terrain of the desert and found their God in its midst.

In 1901, not long after Louis Massignon's visit to J.-K. Huysmans, he was encouraged by his father to travel alone to Algeria. Even at seventeen years old, Massignon was deeply attracted to the beauty of the desert. He wasn't yet consciously connecting his attraction to an experience of the sacred, but rather to his sensitivity to the artistic images of beauty that were so much a part of his life growing up. Despite his pursuit of an intellectual path, the sacred nature of art was not lost on him. He had been thoroughly exposed to the French art world and the religious themes, biblical figures, and medieval images of saints and martyrs, that still attracted artists in late 19th century Western Europe. The longing for transcendence that the arts often represent may be what drew him unconsciously towards the Christian mystics as he began his studies at the Sorbonne. At the time his approach to studying the writings of the great mystics, such as the Spanish Carmelite John of the Cross and the German Meister Eckhart, was his interest in linguistics. It was the use of language, particularly the language of love in literature and mystical writings, that initially caught his attention.

Massignon's childhood interest in North Africa and first trip to Algeria determined his choice of research project for his University diploma. An extensive study of the 16th century geographer of Morocco, Leo Africanus, led to his return to North Africa in 1904 and the study of the Semitic languages Arabic and Hebrew. Like many young people at the age of 20, Massignon seemed to be searching for himself, for a sense of wholeness and individual identity, and a release for his abundant energy. Once again he was drawn to the desert with its beauty and extreme environment which seemed to feed his own longing for transcendence. Thus, he tested his courage with dangerous journeys on horseback and caravans through the desert of Morocco in pursuit of his intellectual project describing the history and geography of the region.

On this journey Massignon discovered a book by the hermit-priest Charles de Foucauld about his exploration of Morocco in 1883. Foucauld had spent a year of adventure traveling in Morocco disguised as a Russian Rabbi. Like the novelist, Huysmans, Foucauld also rediscovered Christianity at the age of 28. He spent the remainder of his life living out his religious vocation in North Africa, growing in his love, understanding, and respect for the Arab and Berber people, and the rigorous life in the desert. Massignon used Foucauld's description of Morocco as a primary source for his thesis and arranged to send a copy to the priest with a letter of thanks when it was later published in Algeria in 1906.

Foucauld's response ended with a blessing: "I offer to God

for you my poor and unworthy prayers, begging Him to bless you, to bless your work and your whole life."[1] Massignon later admitted that he had no faith at the time but somehow accepted what he called, "this poor man's alms"[2] and then forgot the letter altogether in the midst of his activities in Paris.

This chapter begins with the story of Charles de Foucauld, whose life following his adventure in Morocco has become a legend. It is the story of a man who, like many of us today, struggled with his individualistic nature, his workaholic and perfectionistic temperament, and the contradictions and perplexities of his life. His story is of an ordinary man radically changed by his experience of God.

Part One: Charles de Foucauld

Charles-Eugéne de Foucauld was born in Strasbourg, France September 15, 1858 into a family with an impressive number of saints, soldiers, priests and civil servants among their ancestors. His maternal grandfather was a colonel in the French military. His sister, Marie, was born August 13, 1861. Like most children born into French Catholic families at the time, Charles and Marie were introduced to church traditions and devotions by their mother in their early years. Their father, stricken with tuberculosis, was forced to leave his job as an inspector for the Ministry of Water and Forests. In order to avoid exposing his wife and family to his disease, he went to live with his sister, Inès Moitessier.

The family was in a crisis and Charles' mother, who was pregnant again, went with her children to live with her father, Colonel Charles-Gabriel de Morlet. There she died at the age of thirty-four of a miscarriage on March 13, 1864. On August 9th of the same year Charles and Marie lost their father too. The children were entrusted to their maternal grandfather who by then was retired and nearly seventy years old.

We think of becoming an orphan at age six as a tragedy with an impact on the rest of a child's life and can only speculate on how these losses affected Charles' personality. We know that he was a sensitive child, intolerant of teasing. Colonel Morlet was distraught by the death of his daughter. Seeing her resemblance in the face of her son, Charles, he could not resist his young grandson's tears and soon spoiled him. The six year old Charles had a temper and was easily provoked into a rage, a trait he was to struggle with throughout his life.

Fortunately, Charles spent his summer vacations with the Moitessiers and became friends with his cousin Marie who was eight years older than he. She became like a second mother to him. In the midst of this family he was again exposed to the church and religious devotions. Charles saw his cousin attend daily Mass and she showed him the statue of the Sacred Heart that the Moitessier family had donated to the Church.[3] Along with his sister, his cousin Marie remained close to him throughout his life.

Charles was sent to a parochial school in Strasbourg where he received his First Communion. When the French went to war his grandfather sought refuge in Berne, Switzerland. Charles later wrote that age 10 was the worst time in his childhood. After the war his grandfather chose to retain his French nationality which meant they could not return to Strasbourg. Instead they moved to Nancy where Charles first began to make less effort in school and soon lost his faith as well. He preferred solitude and reading books of his own choice. Studies in philosophy raised his doubts and the intellectual atmosphere of relativity at the end of the 19th century in France influenced him as well. As a teenager he only knew that he did not know if there was a God or not. He came to the conclusion that human beings were not capable of knowing the truth.[4]

In 1874, when his cousin, Marie Moitessier, was married Charles felt betrayed because Marie had been like a second mother to him. Now she would be less emotionally available. Although he got through his studies he was inclined to make less and less effort. In his letters he reveals the bitterness he felt at the time and how he began to come face to face with his own faults. This self-scrutiny also became a life-long trait.[5] When he passed his first baccalauréat his grandfather wanted him to go to a Polytechnical School but Charles resisted, choosing an easier school called l'Ecole de Saint Cyr in Paris. He wrote that at 17 he had never been in such a bad state of mind. He described himself as egotistical, vain, impious, and lazy. He ignored the many letters from his grandfather causing the old man great distress.[6] As for his faith, he later wrote that he did not believe in God for 13 years.[7]

In his second year at Saint Cyr he was suddenly called back to Nancy with his sister, Marie. Their grandfather was dying. Colonel Morlet died February 3, 1878. Charles lost interest in taking care of himself and threw himself into a self-destructive and dissolute life-style for the remainder of the year. His depression was understandable. A few months after he graduated from Saint Cyr something changed in him. At the age of twenty he decided to take up life with a vengeance. He was determined to enjoy life, to live as intensely as possible.[8]

In 1876 Charles entered military academy almost being denied entrance due to obesity. He graduated as one of the last in his class, just as he had entered. A photograph at the time shows a thick-necked, round-faced young man with eyes nearly disappearing into his fleshy face. One day this portrait would be transformed into the legendary Charles de Foucauld, described by his biographer as a small, energetic and wiry man with a celestial smile and splendid brilliant eyes.[9] But he had yet to get through cavalry school in Saumur where he lavishly squandered his inheritance on dinners, parties, and only the best cigars. His reputation finally made it impossible for him to even get a room. Even so, he finished his training as a lieutenant and spent the year in a small town with his regiment, continuing to go from party to party. In December 1880 he was sent to Algeria with his comrades in the 4th cavalry regiment.

Here, in Sétif, Africa he became involved with a young French woman who had arrived there at the same time. Defying his superiors he willfully continued to live with this young woman and finally was asked to take a temporary leave, returning to Evian, France. Isolated from his friends and family with nothing to do he heard that his regiment was being sent into battle. Something finally caught Charles' attention. He wanted to join his comrades, enter into the danger, and fight for France. For the first time Charles became a soldier and a leader. He also discovered that he admired the Arabs and determined to study this mysterious and unknown people when the uprising was over. At 24 years old Charles petitioned the military to dismiss him from active duty and he returned to Algeria.[10]

Just as his need for an inner sense of autonomy, solitude, and some sense of liberation caused him to defy his superiors and leave the military in 1881, so this same desire governed his choice to once again abandon his military career to pursue his passion to study the Arabs and explore the vast, silent, and mysterious experience of the desert. However, his habit of lavishly spending his inheritance caused his aunt to intervene and ask his cousin, M. De Latouche, to become his financial advisor. He was called back to Nancy. This time he agreed to limit his expenses and surprisingly accepted the small sum of 350 francs a month which would also pay for his studies in Arabic.[11]

Jean François Six suggests that Charles needed to be a hero. He was searching for his own identity and initiative by testing his personal courage and wanted to prove to himself and to others that he was capable of great actions.[12] Charles wanted to be the first European to explore Morocco. He once again returned to Algeria where he diligently began to learn Arabic and prepare himself for a rigorous journey.

It is difficult more than one hundred years later to imagine the enormity of Charles' courage in taking on this plan to explore Morocco. No European had succeeded before him. The regions that he wished to explore were only accepting of, and familiar with, Muslim Arabs and Jews. The people were fearful and antagonistic towards Christian Europeans who were seen as invaders, conquerors, and foreigners. There was a great chance of real danger from pirates, and bands of thieves were known to be in the region. He was advised therefore to take on a disguise, either Arab or Jew. He chose to impersonate a Jewish Rabbi because it allowed him to travel unnoticed and gave him more freedom to make his observations and take copious daily notes. He wrote that no one would speak to a poor Jew other than his "cousins, as the Moroccan Jews called themselves." They gave him details of the region and helpful directions.[13] He had a Jewish guide who also helped him to avoid suspicion. He left Algeria June 30, 1883 determined to succeed no matter what it took. His journey took 11 months. He wrote to his sister who was concerned for his safety, "When we leave saying that we will do something we must not return without having done it."[14] He was profoundly affected by his experience in Morocco to the end of his life.

After his arduous journey, Charles returned to Algeria. There he had an experience to which many of us can relate. He discovered that nothing had changed. He was still impatient, passionately driven to live intensely, unable to tolerate the limitations of time and daily life, easily bored, and still imprisoned by his own willpower. After 15 days in Algeria he returned to Paris on June 17, 1884. He then went to the Château du Tuguet, the Moitessier's summer home. His cousin Marie was also there.[15]

While still in Algeria he confronted the aspects of himself that seemed to him to be the same as always, yet in fact, after six weeks with his family the effects of his journey began to be noticed by others. Renewing his friendship with Marie lifted his spirits and he was noticeably calmer and more reflective.

After fulfilling his obligatory month in the army reserves in September, Charles returned to Africa and remained there for the next ten months only returning to France briefly to attend his sister's wedding on December 30th, 1884. While working on compiling his notes from his Moroccan exploration he met the daughter of Commander Titre who he was consulting about his plans for another African journey into the desert. For a short time he considered marrying this young woman but took the advice of his cousin, Marie, who cautioned him not to make a hasty decision. His brother-in-law received the gold medal for him from the French Geographic Society for his remarkable work in Morocco, while Charles continued to perfect his notes for publication. He wanted to travel to portions of the Algerian Sahara and Tunisia to include a comparison with his findings in Morocco before completing his manuscript, *La Reconnaisance au Moroc*. He completed this journey by January 1886 and returned to Paris with the intention of staying through the Spring. He rented an apartment in the rue de Miromesnil not far from the hotel where his cousin Marie was staying with her mother.[16]

Although Charles admittedly had no faith and continued to believe that human beings could not know the truth, the issue of God in his own life was perpetually in question. He could not avoid being affected by his exposure to the religious practices of both Jews and Muslims in Morocco. In his studies of Arabic he read the teachings of the Prophet in the Koran: "There is one God to whom all are subjected, who knows everything, and is worthy of praise."[17] Five times a day Charles heard the Muslim call to prayer and saw rows of people humbly kneeling right where they were before their God. Something in this experience woke him up to the grandeur of God and a need to be somehow purified. While in Paris he made a decision to be chaste. Moreover, he continued to sleep on a simple mat in his apartment just as he had done in the desert.

His conversion experience had begun. He knew that he did not want to repeat his past mistakes and searched for a way to become virtuous. The example of his cousin Marie's sincere Catholic devotion and the effect of his family's warm acceptance of him deeply impressed him. Marie was intelligent and took her spiritual director's advice to heart. Abbé Huvelin knew that the human soul is not converted by preaching but rather by loving.[18] Charles searched the texts of philosophy to find his sense of morality and was once again disappointed. He finally understood that his sadness did not disappear when he studied philosophy and science, or even when his hard work led to success and recognition. One day he came across some pages in the book by Bossuet, *Elévations sur les Mystères* that his cousin

Marie had given him on the day of his First Communion. He thought that here at least in this dogmatic book he would find something about moral teachings if not the truth he was seeking.[19] However faith in God continued to elude him despite his desire to be virtuous. He stayed in Paris in the midst of his silently religious and loving family atmosphere for six months, then returned for a month to Tunisia to verify the final geographic observations for his book.

In this short time away from his family something changed for Charles. He began to think that if all these intelligent, virtuous people like his cousin Marie and her family and friends were faithful Christians that perhaps it wasn't absurd after all.[20] Moreover they were genuinely happy and generous with their affection. Perhaps this had something to do with their faith. When he returned to Paris he found himself inexplicably drawn to silently sitting in churches, always praying the same prayer, "My God, if You exist let me know it."[21] A solitary figure sitting for hours in the immense stone churches of Paris, surrounded by religious statues and stain glass images symbolic of Christian faith in God, Charles found himself thinking that if the truth could not be found anywhere else on earth, not even in any philosophical system, perhaps it could be found in the religion of the Church after all.[22] He began to wonder if he should find a Catholic priest to instruct him in the same way that he had found a teacher when he wanted to study Arabic.

One day, late in October 1886, Charles was sitting in the parish Church of Saint Augustin when he saw a priest take his place in the confessional. Charles followed him, but rather than kneeling, as was the custom, he simply said that he wasn't there to make his confession because he had no faith, but asked the priest if he could receive instruction in Catholicism. The priest's response to Charles was direct and simple. He instructed Charles to kneel and make his confession. Charles obeyed. Then Charles was told to go to the Mary altar and receive communion. The priest was Abbé Huvelin, a man who deeply understood the needs of the human soul. He was a very kind and humble man but he was also very perceptive and uncompromising in his spiritual direction of the many, often famous people, who sought his advice.[23]

Abbé Huvelin invited Charles to assist him at the celebration of Mass everyday and encouraged him to receive daily communion as well, a practice that was controversial at the time. Father Huvelin's understanding of the mystery of the Eucharist was a foreshadowing of current views in the church. Charles received the benefit of this man's insights which were 100 years before their time.

Years later in a letter to his friend Henry de Castries written on August 14, 1901 and in a long meditation written on a retreat at Nazareth in November 1897, Charles was able to see in retrospect how he was being pushed towards God. The fact that he was searching so desperately was in itself the Spirit of God working within him. God was there in his need for solitude, in the hours he sat alone in church, in his anguish and desire for the truth. He even recognized how his cousin Marie's kindness towards him and her silent religious devotion demonstrated the way that we are often called to God through the beauty of other souls.[24] He remained forever grateful to Abbé Huvelin who became his friend and spiritual guide for 24 years until Abbé Huvelin's death in 1910. Charles wrote of God: "You put me under the wings of this Saint, and I stayed there."[25]

On that day in October when he made his confession and received communion after 13 years, Charles felt he was blessed by God. He understood that he had been given one grace after another. From the moment that he believed that there was a God he knew that he could not do otherwise than live only for Him. His religious vocation began at the same hour as his faith.[26] He realized how God had been present at every choice in his life mercifully saving him throughout. From this point on this story is about the love affair of Charles de Foucauld with his God.

Receiving daily communion Charles' desire to give himself entirely to God became more and more intense. He now knew that he wanted a vocation to religious life. He was impatient to accomplish his goal but Abbé Huvelin understood that discerning God's will requires patience, self-denial and time. Charles' pride in accomplishments and heroic adventures must be replaced by a desire for God alone. The wise priest insisted that Charles wait. In fact, he would wait for three more years. During this time he read many spiritual books and immersed himself in scripture. He found himself drawn to monastic life and the Religious Orders founded by those who shared the experience of his own beloved desert.

On February 4, 1888 *La Reconnaissance au Maroc* was published. Despite its immediate success and his many invitations to become a celebrity, Charles experienced something false and vain in it and began to feel a vast difference between what he described as the "perfect Gospel life" and the life most people were living.[27] To others he seemed to be suffering from some sickness and he admitted his lack of inner peace in a letter to a friend.[28] Charles was profoundly affected by Abbé Huvelin's sermons which presented an image of Jesus as the poorest of the poor. Although he wasn't imagining great explorations any longer, he seemed to long for the desert itself. It was not yet clear to him where God was leading him and how he could imitate Jesus.

At the request of his spiritual mentor he made a pilgimage to the Holy Land from the end of November 1888 to the beginning of February 1889. During this time his vocation became clear. On this journey from Jerusalem to Jesus' birthplace in Bethlehem and to Nazareth, Charles came face to face with the mystery of the Cross. On January 10, 1889, in the city of Nazareth Charles became aware of the hidden life of Jesus; those years of growing up in Nazareth that we know so little about. For the rest of his life Charles de Foucauld followed this path of the hidden life of Jesus of Nazareth as he perceived it, a life of simplicity, poverty and humility.

On return to France he spent months going on one retreat after another in different monastic communities struggling to discern where God was leading him. At last he wrote to his sister that he had found a great sense of inner peace. He had decided to serve God in love and obscurity by entering a Trappist monastery, a strict Cistercian Religious Order vowed to silence, solitude, and prayer.[29] On January 10, 1890 Charles became a novice at Our Lady of the Snows in a remote region of France high in the mountains. True to his character, Charles wanted to make an even more extreme sacrifice by choosing to live far away from the family he loved and the spiritual guide on whom he relied. Several months after he received his habit, taking the religious name brother Marie-Abéric, Charles was sent to Syria. On July 10, 1890 he entered the small and very poor Cistercian priory in Cheïkhle, near Akbès, Syria called Our Lady of the Sacred Heart. There he began his life in imitation of Jesus, "the poor and humble workman of Nazareth."[30]

But Charles' demons were still with him. Even this poor monastery did not seem poor enough for his image of the carpenter of Nazareth. He struggled to accept the vow of obedience to his superiors, just as he had struggled with authority when he was a soldier. Brotherly love was hard to feel towards his monastic brothers and their communal life. He was a harsh judge of others in his intense desire to live in poverty and obscurity. Although Charles was clearly not temperamentally suited for community life, he remained at Sacred Heart for seven and a half years. At the age of 33, on February 2, 1892 Charles made his first vows to the Order. Shortly afterwards he was ordered to study for the priesthood. He obeyed, but internally he felt misunderstood. He was seeking to remain the last, the least, the most humble and poor. He thought the priesthood would place him above others. Most of all he longed for solitude. As severe as life was at Our Lady of the Sacred Heart, Charles felt it was not austere enough. He longed to form a small congregation of like-minded souls.

After only three years as a monk he began to write out his dream of a rule for a new Religious Order. They would live among the most abandoned in non-Christian countries. He wanted to save souls while remaining the poorest and unrecognized of them.[31] He wanted to leave the Order, to disappear more completely than he had already done in Syria. "Is this desire from God, or from a demon, or my imagination?" he asked his confessor at Sacred Heart. He was told, "Don't think about it anymore. Wait peacefully because if your desire is from God the occasion for its birth will happen."[32] He wrote to Abbé Huvelin who knew Charles well and understood his intense desire for perfection. He also knew how the most gifted souls could throw themselves in good faith into their vision and perish.[33] He encouraged him to finish his studies. Charles asked for permission to leave the Order but was told that he should spend the next two years finishing his studies in Rome. They wanted to be sure that his desires were not a disguise for his own pride.[34]

Charles went to Rome. Before taking his final vows he had to decide whether to stay in the Order or leave. He sent a copy of his ideas for a rule for his Little Brothers of Jesus to Abbé Huvelin who found them idealistic and so impossibly severe that they were unlivable. He advised Charles that if he did leave the Order he should live in solitude, as he envisioned, near to a religious community. He encouraged him not to try to establish a rule for others that was bound to fail. Just days before he would have made his final vows Charles received permission to leave the Trappist Order. At Abbé Huvelin's suggestion he went back to Nazareth intending to live in poverty beside a convent, asking only for spiritual resources. Charles was 38 years old when he arrived in Nazareth on March 5, 1897 exhausted from walking through Galilee for 12 days. He had chosen to dress in a long tunic with a hood, cinched with a leather belt from which a string of Rosary beads hung. He wore blue workman's trousers and sandals.[35] This strange outfit attracted attention even though Charles imagined that if he took the disguise of a poor working class pilgrim he would be able to achieve the solitary and hidden life of prayer he longed for.

Charles arranged to live in a small hut on the property near the convent of a Franciscan Order of Sisters called the Poor Clares. He asked only for bread and water and time to pray, offering to serve the Sisters in any way they needed. It soon became clear to the Sisters that Charles was not very talented at carpentry or masonry.[36] But he did have a gift for drawing and gave the Sisters images of the Holy Family, copies of Icons of Saint Francis and a series of miniature religious drawings which he thought would edify the Sister's prayer life.

In time the Sisters learned about his past, that he came from an aristocratic family and had been a lieutenant in the French cavalry who had undergone a transforming conversion experience. Charles began to be thought of as a Holy Man. He spent three years filling his days with some small tasks for the Sisters, spiritual reading and long hours in prayer. He barely ate or slept and kept himself awake through the night before the altar by writing in his diary. In fact, most of his spiritual writing dates from these years in Nazareth. It was here that Charles found his desire increasing more and more to imitate Jesus and immerse himself in God. For Charles, who still retained the instincts of a French lieutenant, to attempt to live as poorly as he imagined Jesus the carpenter of Nazareth did was humbling, even though he had little idea of what the poor working class men, women and children around him truly suffered. He would learn that later.

After one year his ideas about the priesthood began to change. He was encouraged by the Mother Superior of the Poor Clares in Jerusalem, but it took two more years for him to return to France and take the year necessary to finish his requirements for ordination. During this year starting on September 29, 1900 Charles realized that his life in his beloved Holy Land at Nazareth was not where he was meant to be. He wanted to work for God, declaring the Gospel through his life. One month before his ordination he remembered Morocco, the one place on earth that he had experienced millions of people who were poor and non-Christians, and who had no priests.

On June 9, 1901 Brother Charles was ordained a priest. At the age of 42 Père Charles went back to the desert in Africa, establishing himself in Beni Abbès, Algeria, an oasis near the border of Morocco recently conquered by the French. Beni Abbès was an oasis in a river valley with thousands of palm trees, bordered by tiers of sand dunes on one side, and a rocky plateau which stretched out to the mountainous frontier of Morocco on the other. Charles chose a remote spot at the edge of the rocky terrain to build his palm-roofed chapel and small dwelling. He was welcomed by the French garrison which shared the oasis with two separate tribal villages and their slave laborers. Charles came face to face with French colonialism and the religion of Islam.

In time his hermetic way of life turned into a life of serving hundreds a day. They were soldiers, Algerians and slaves, men, women and children. They came seeking food and medicine, or a place to sleep, or spiritual advice. He even went to serve the military when there were uprisings and wounded to whom he brought the Sacraments. He accepted everyone, Christians, Muslims, Jews, slaves and nonreligious as brothers and sisters. His house became known as the "fraternity".[37] Charles began to understand more and more clearly that he would draw more to Christ by treating everyone equally and living a holy life than by preaching to them. Abbé Huvelin's example during his early years in Paris served him well.

He struggled with the dichotomy between his desire to be a "universal brother" to all and his calling to prayer and solitude. There was never enough time to pray, or, when he tried at the end of a long day, he would fall asleep from exhaustion.[38] Charles petitioned against the buying and selling of slaves and risked alienating the new antireligious Republic in France by proposing a missionary project for Morocco. He continued to dream throughout his life of a community of Little Brothers and Sisters of the Sacred Heart of Jesus serving God with him in the desert.[39] He envisioned French schools, nursing facilities, and conversions. He kept up an extensive correspondence with his Superiors and Trappist Brothers at Our Lady of the Snows, his family and some close friends. Although he asked the French Apostolic Prefect of the Sahara, the White Father's Community and the Trappists for others to join him in his dream of a religious community, he finally simply prayed for one companion.

From 1904 to 1905 Brother Charles agreed to a journey with his close friend, Major Lapperine, to help establish peace between the French and the native Algerian Touareg tribes in the region, known as the Hoggar. They crossed the desert from north to south far from the Moroccan border. For the year they lived as nomads and Charles learned the Touareg language. The Touareg were nomads living in small tribal groups throughout the dry region around the base of the high stony mountain range of the Hoggar. A river flowed mostly under the surface of the dry river bed allowing for cultivation of wheat, barley and millet. The Touareg were thought to be descendants of the Berbers with their light skin, hair and eyes. Unlike the Arabs of Beni Abbès who practiced a more traditional Islam, the Touareg were less dogmatic about their religion. On this journey Brother Charles met the chief of the tribe, Moussa ag Amastane, who negotiated peace with the French military for the area. Brother Charles found himself imagining that here he would truly be a missionary priest, far from the French troops, other Christians and even another priest.

With the permission of the Apostolic Prefect of the Sahara, Père Guerin, and the encouragement of Major Lapperine, Brother Charles agreed to move into the Hoggar to the small Touareg village of Tamanrasset on September 3, 1905. He built a reed hut and his chapel on the edge of the village inhabited by the Touareg and the black-skinned Harratine who labored in the fields for them. Life in Tamanrasset was very different than in Beni Abbès. Here Brother Charles was a hermit. The nomads and villagers did not visit him. Instead he went out to them, slowly building their trust and finally their affection. True to his perfectionistic nature, Brother Charles stuck to his daily rule of devotions and prayer, and spent the rest of his time on the tedious and demanding task of learning the language of the Touareg. He translated the Gospels and then went to work creating a Touareg/French dictionary and grammar. He believed with his whole heart that other missionaries would follow him and need this guide. He also came to love these people and their culture, spending hours memorizing their poetry and oral traditions and translating them into French. He taught the natives French as well.

The mail took months to arrive but Brother Charles wrote back immediately to all his correspondents. In time he established very close friends among the Touareg including their chief, Moussa, and the Harratine people, buying a slave's freedom whenever that was possible. There was drought, and the nomads moved on leaving only a few of the poorest villagers. Because the Catholic Mass is meant to be communal, Père Charles was not permitted to celebrate Mass for six years. He continued his devotion and regimen of prayer until one of the priests from the White Fathers Order took the opportunity on a trip to Rome to ask that the hermit/priest be permitted to celebrate Mass alone. On January 31, 1908 Père Charles heard the news that the request was granted.

Just at that moment Brother Charles became sick, probably from fatigue and malnutrition, and the Touareg villagers took care of him, collecting all the milk from the goats in the area to bring to him. The news of his illness traveled and eventually Major Lapperine also came to his aid with supplies. Brother Charles realized that he was getting older and worried that there would be no one to replace him. He had built enough monastic cells in his hermitage at Beni Abbès for twenty monks, and established his hermitage in Tamanrasset as well.

On a retreat in 1909 he began to formulate an idea for a Third Order, or Association, made up of French and Algerian Christians who would pray for the Muslims in the French colonies in Africa. He created a simple rule that could include people from all walks of life joined together by a missionary spirit of prayer. This was an example of Brother Charles' vision of the Catholic Christian concept of the Communion of Saints. In February he received permission to make a short trip to France to visit his family and present his Association to Mgr. Bonnet, the Bishop of Viviers and Mgr. Livinhac, the Superior General of the White Fathers. His idea was approved.

Brother Charles built still another hermitage high in the mountains. In 1911 he spent five months in this solitary place amidst the nomads creating a 2000 page Touareg/French dictionary and 800 pages of Touareg poems, proverbs, legends and traditions. He wanted to do something good for the people he had come to love.[40] Like many workaholics he told himself that he must finish this work to have more time to serve the people, and for prayer and spiritual reading. He had laid the ground for his mission but had very few converts. His greatest desire was to save souls in imitation of Jesus.

In 1913 Brother Charles went for another visit to France to try to establish his Association and was able to bring a young friend, Uksem Son of Shikkat, to France. Then the First World War began. Brother Charles was 55 years old. He remained in Tamanrasset planning to stay there until there was peace in Europe. Seven of his Trappist Brothers from Our Lady of the Snows lost their lives at the front. A band of Muslims from various tribes called the Senoussi took advantage of the war to fight against the French. There were also bands of pillagers in the area but Brother Charles felt that the Touareg were calm and trusted their loyalty to the French should there be any attacks on Tamanrasset. He did begin to build a solid fortress for himself which he envisioned would serve to protect the Touareg in the area if necessary. Meanwhile the French military built a fort 50 kilometers from Tamanrasset

From his many letters it is clear that he sent his military advice to the front and received news from the generals, colonels, and majors some of whom were his friends from school. Throughout, he wrote of his spiritual vision of the role of the French in relation to the native people in the African colonies. He believed that the beauty of French civilization was a gift to be shared and that as Christians they were bound to befriend and insure the health and well being of the people, as he did. They should learn about the native culture, language and customs with the goal of gaining their trust and overcoming their natural fear of the French foreigners by showing Christian love and respect. It was an idealistic vision for the French colonies grounded in his own passionate love of Christianity. On June 23, 1916 he moved into his fortress for safety. It was here that Brother Charles of Jesus' mission came to an abrupt and tragic end.

On December 1, 1916, the first Friday of the month dedicated to the Sacred Heart of Jesus, the Senoussi led a band of raiders including some Touareg into Tamanrasset. One of them knocked on the door of the fortress saying he was bringing the mail. When Brother Charles opened the door he was pulled out, tied hand and foot, and thrown to his knees. When two soldiers intending to pay a visit to the priest unexpectedly appeared they were shot and killed causing one of the guards to fire the shot that also killed Brother Charles. The beloved hermit/priest was 57 years old.[41]

Brother Charles of Jesus gave his life for France and for his God. He was a French aristocrat and soldier who loved his country and he was a product of his time. He never thought to question the colonial position of France any more than he questioned his faith that Jesus died to save every soul in the world. The extreme nature of his personality allowed him to believe that living a holy Christian life in the midst of non-Christians, accepting every person, loving them, and serving them would bring them to Christ. He came to see Christ in everyone and it is clear that his own life was entirely transformed by his passionate love of God.

Part Two: A Parallel Spiritual Journey

Louis Massignon was 23 years old in 1906 when he sent his publication of his study of Morocco to the desert priest and received in return a blessing of his work and his life. He had no way of knowing that this forgotten communication with Father Charles de Foucauld was the beginning of a lifelong connection. Many years later in a talk about the hermit priest in 1959, Massignon spoke of his relationship to Foucauld as a "constellation of tiny weblike threads between our two vocations and our destinies."[42]

At 23 Louis, like the young Charles, understood human freedom and willpower as an exemption from the need for divine grace in his life. He only knew that he had a thirst for knowledge and a fascination for the Middle East. A young French actress had also apparently occupied his attention for the past two years. This caused his father to arrange for him to take a position in Cairo for a year at the French Institute of Oriental Archeology after he received his diploma in Arabic. It was appealing to Louis to take a year to perfect the language and to study the religion of Islam.[43] Like most young people in their early twenties he was open to experiencing life and ready for adventure.

On the ship to Alexandria Louis met a young man from an aristocratic Spanish family who had converted to Islam from Christianity. He entered into a homosexual relationship with Luis de Cuadra and experienced a year of passionate, desperate, and sometimes violent adventures. At the same time he felt a sense of moral conflict, inner emptiness and anxiety, and struggled with his thirst for something beyond himself that he could not yet name. Luis de Cuadra was five years older than Louis and led his friend into the midst of Arab night life in Cairo. Dressed as natives, they sought out forbidden areas of the city.

But Luis de Cuadra also encouraged Louis' intellectual pursuit and understanding of the religion of Islam. Louis was drawn to the Sufi mystics while he continued to immerse himself in Arab culture and philosophy. March 24, 1907 was a date that Louis never forgot because it was the day that his friend pointed out a passage by a little known Islamic mystic called al-Hallaj in a book by the Persian author, Farid-ud-Din' Attar called *The Memorial of the Saints*.[44] "Two moments of adoration suffice in love, but the preliminary ablution must be made in blood." Later Louis wrote that these words by Hallaj woke him up. Like a revelation he suddenly felt the "meaning of sin" and a "piercing desire for purity…"[45] This year in Cairo would strike him years later as a necessary "season in Hell" that would affect the rest of his life. He wanted to know more about

Hallaj and was intrigued by the legends that surrounded the Sufi mystic. But it was more than that. Hallaj was crucified as a heretic for preaching about his experience of God's love in public. It was the image of the Muslim martyr, crucified as Jesus was crucified, that held Louis captive. Despite his earlier intention to pursue his interest in Egyptian archeology, he now decided to make Hallaj the subject of his doctoral thesis. He returned to Paris.

In Paris he was offered an opportunity to take on an archeological mission in Mesopotamia. Similar to Charles and his exploration of Morocco, the 24 year old Louis was going on an uncharted journey into a part of the Ottoman Empire that was distrustful of Europeans. He was expected to visit historic sites and document them in an unknown region that was likely to be dangerous. As he was to write later in his life, he was driven by his passion to understand the Arabs and Islam very much like the young Charles de Foucauld.[46] This was an opportunity to go to Baghdad and to pursue his research where the tenth century mystic Hallaj once lived and was put to death. But he did not share this goal for his journey with the general who assigned him to this mission.

Louis left Marseille on November 7, 1907 on a ship called the Luristan. He was headed into an area of extreme political unrest and in Baghdad the French Consul became his safety and avenue to permission from the Turkish government for his work and his living arrangements. He made the unusual request for a European to live in the Muslim community. Once again he dressed as an Arab as he had done in Cairo and lived near a prominent Muslim archeologist and his family. He perceived himself as their guest and was grateful for their hospitality. The Alussys were devout Muslims who considered Hallaj marginal at best, and his doctrine of union with God questionable if not heretical, despite the legends and popular devotion surrounding the mystic. As traditional Hanbalite Muslims they believed that God cannot be known by humans other than by faith alone.

Louis' host, Hajj 'Ali challenged his agnosticism by the

example of his faith and the two men engaged in many conversations about religion. Louis made the decision not to embarrass his hosts in any way and "forced himself to be chaste" despite his longing for his friend in Cairo. He visited a Carmelite priest in Baghdad as well who admired the young Frenchman's intelligence and knowledge of Arabic and the Muslim mystics. Father Anastase-Marie de Saint Elie was only surprised that Louis had less knowledge of the Christian mystics.[47] Louis was being prepared unknowingly for his own conversion experience. He was learning about Islam as his new friend Hajj 'Ali experienced it, in the depth of his being. He was also influenced by his search for Hallaj who was known as "the one whose desire for God burned in his heart."

While he was earnestly gathering archeological data in Baghdad for his mission he was also collecting information for his thesis on Hallaj. But his assignment was to explore areas outside of Baghdad and specifically to collect data for the French before two German archeologists were able to do so. In fact these men reported him to the Turkish authorities as a spy. With the help of the French Consul and his prominent friends Louis prepared a caravan and an itinerary to complete his assignment.[48] On March 22, 1908 he began his journey to the holy places and ruins of the region. Despite an attack by bandits he continued to travel alone except for his native escorts for miles in the desert through the month of April. One of these escorts began to call him "effeminate" which caused Louis to confront him angrily. The man left the caravan with a comrade taking the money for supplies with them. When the caravan reached a place called Kut, Louis reported the theft to the authorities. He was unable to get cash because his identity was questioned and ultimately he found himself trapped in the midst of the political intrigue that led to the Turkish revolution. The Turkish officials were anxious to get him out of the area and he was finally given a ticket on a steamer back to Baghdad. Louis was unsure of exactly what had happened as details of the political situation were unknown to him.

On board the steamer he found himself surrounded by

Turkish and Iraqi passengers and began to feel they were staring at him and imagined their judgment. He was sure the rumors about him started by his wayward escort in the desert had followed him aboard the ship. In fact one man whispered to him that he had been accused of being a spy and a collaborator in an assassination attempt on the life of an important Turkish official. Louis began to panic. He was sure his life was in danger. In his fear and growing anxiety he prayed the first words that came to him in Arabic, "God, God help my weakness!"[49]

Louis seemed to succumb to his fear and began to behave in ways that the captain of the ship later described as "crazy." First he appealed to the captain for safety and gave up his revolver. Then apparently he became convinced that he had failed in his mission and began to experience terrible anxiety about his moral behavior as well. He was sure that he was going to die at the hands of those who accused him of being a spy. He unsuccessfully tried to escape when the ship made a stop, and was then tied up and confined to the captain's cabin. Louis began to feel desperate. Years later he wrote," I began to suffer from myself....look at how I was ending up after four and a half years of amorality....Dying in a terrible situation; my family would be happy to forget me...."[50]

He decided to commit suicide and wounded himself with a knife, then panicked when he saw his own blood. He was treated by the ship's doctor who later described him as becoming increasingly "agitated" in between short periods of sleep. Louis was feeling caught in an impossible trap, unable to control his own destiny even by taking his own life. Sometime in the midst of his overwhelming despair, on May 2nd or 3rd, he had an experience of a mysterious presence that he later called the "Visitation of the Stranger." It left him changed for the rest of his life. He was astonished, left speechless and powerless and so deeply affected that he could not remember his own name. He was left with the certainty that he would return to Paris unharmed.

Louis arrived in Baghdad sick with malaria and was hospitalized there. During his illness and his recuperation he continued to experience incidents that he called "supernatural." He later described four episodes in which he went from a profound sense of self-condemnation and being judged, to a feeling of liberation and pardon for the sins he had committed in his life. He felt spiritually reborn by God's mercy and compassion.[51] He felt he had been judged as at the moment of death and saved from hell. Now he knew the reality of sin and understood what pain awaits those who are lost if they do not become reconciled to God. He felt he had a debt to pay, and while he knew the debt had already been paid by this "Stranger" he also knew that in some way he must continue to atone for his faults.[52] Louis had found his God in the Catholic faith.

The young 25 year old Louis Massignon, in his striving for independence from his family, had befriended the convert to Islam, Luis de Cuadra and become close to the Allussy family who prayed Muslim prayers for him during his illness. He had lived for four years immersed in Arab culture and become fascinated with the Sufi mystic, Hallaj. He seemed destined to one day turn to Islam. And yet, as a result of an inexpressible experience of the Divine, Louis' conversion experience caused him to embrace the Roman Catholic religion of his childhood. Louis was convinced that the tenth century Muslim mystic, Hallaj, had mysteriously intervened in his life, drawing him to Baghdad. He was also sure that his conversion experience was due in part to the prayers of J.-K. Huysmans, his mother and the desert priest, Charles de Foucauld.

Massignon returned to France and with renewed energy completed his reports on his journey to Mesopotamia. Meanwhile, he began compiling his notes for his thesis on Hallaj. He had no idea at the time that his work on the life and mystical experience of the tenth century Muslim would become an intense relationship that would continue to inspire his own ongoing conversion experience for the rest of his life. Hallaj was his first "intercessor" and the one who led him home to his Christian roots. Moreover, he envisioned Hallaj as a martyr whose intense love of God and the Muslim community caused him to willingly sacrifice his life. Huysmans' story of Saint

Lydwine had perhaps planted the seed for Massignon's understanding of mystical substitution but the Muslim mystic's story allowed him to embrace it as the foundation for his own spirituality. He saw in Hallaj the image of Christ, who was the first in a litany of saints who followed him to substitute his life for the salvation of the world.

During this time Massignon went on the first of a lifetime of pilgrimages to the sites dedicated to these saints as he wrestled with his own vocation as a Christian. He too wanted to be chosen as a witness for God. Louis made a vow to give himself to God in thanksgiving for his new found faith. He felt indebted to his Muslim friends, the Allusys and silently offered himself to God for their conversion. He also felt indebted to his Spanish Muslim friend, Luis de Cuadra, for introducing him to Hallaj and wanted to "save" him. He wrote Luis with his intention to offer his life to God so that his friend would return to Christianity. Luis de Cuadra accepted the offer but nevertheless continued to embrace Islam.

Massignon sought out other practicing Christians to share his experience and guide his journey. He began to correspond with Paul Claudel, a French diplomat and poet who also had a conversion experience. Claudel became a close friend and confidant. Massignon also wrote for the second time to Charles de Foucauld, sensing the desert priest's role in his extraordinary experience. Here were two intense personalities meeting on the ground of their shared faith journeys. Both were turned around in their lives by an experience of the Divine and from then on became passionately committed to the spiritual quest. Foucauld wrote back that he was coming to Paris. In February 1909 Massignon met Foucauld for the first time in his family's home. One night they went together to pray as Foucauld always prayed, sitting vigil for the whole night before the Blessed Sacrament at the Sacre Coeur overlooking the city of Paris. When the priest returned to Africa the two began a correspondence that lasted until Foucauld's death in 1916. The desert priest was getting older and longed to mentor one other person who would one day replace him in Tamanrasset. He began to envision the 25 year old Louis Massignon as the companion for whom he had prayed for many years.

Massignon was searching for his spiritual vocation and simultaneously for his direction as a scholar. Foucauld invited him to come to the desert and join him in his studies of the Touareg people and suggested he eventually study for the priesthood as well. The invitation became a large part of Massignon's personal struggle to choose his life path. He had always been drawn to the desert, and now longed to somehow dedicate his life entirely to God, and yet he was also an unusually talented scholar and linguist. He wrote Foucauld that he had to finish the two theses required for his doctorate before he could make a decision. Meanwhile he continued to share his spiritual struggles in his letters to the priest. He spent the year intently pursuing his academic interests, giving a talk on Muslim Saints in Baghdad and attending the 15th International Congress of Orientalists in Copenhagen. He was beginning to gain a reputation as an international scholar.[53]

Massignon returned to Cairo as a student of philosophy at a university and continued to work on his thesis on Hallaj and complete the publication of his manuscript *Mission en Mesopotamie*. Foucauld understood his need to return to Cairo but also warned him of the difficulties he was likely to face there. In his letters to Claudel Massignon confided how his return to Cairo tempted him to return to his former way of life and how he struggled to hold on to his new found faith experience. He was being pulled in too many directions at once. Foucauld sent him a Touareg grammar and dictionary. Massignon wrote to Claudel that he would have liked to believe that he could be the person that Foucauld imagined, selflessly offering his life to God in the desert. Claudel heard his confusion and wrote to encourage him to consider joining the priest even for a short time. He wrote: "The opinion of a saint has more weight than empty words. What a unique opportunity for you to be able to live in the shadow of such a man!"[54]

In 1910 Massignon returned to Paris still undecided about his future. In 1911 Père Foucauld returned to Paris. He went to say Mass at the Church of Saint Augustine where Abbé Huvelin had so wisely guided him back to the Church so many years before. He invited Massignon to assist him. Once again Massignon was hoping to spend time with the priest in the Hoggar after he finished writing his books. Foucauld sent him explicit travelling instructions for the journey to Tamanrasset. Massignon expected to complete his thesis by January 1912 and thought he would finally be ready for a commitment to go to the desert. But in fact, he continued to hesitate. He was still torn between his inner longings and his intellectual leanings.[55]

During this time Massignon made a pilgrimage to the shrine of Our Lady of LaSalette in memory of J.-K. Huysmans' conversion experience there. He met Père Daniel Fontaine who was the novelist's last confessor. With the pressure from his family to marry and his spiritual director Père Poulin's wariness of Foucauld, Massignon turned to Fontaine to help him make the decision.

Massignon presented a paper at the 16th International Congress of Orientalists in Athens. He spoke about Hallaj and his ecstatic cry, "I am the Truth" that eventually led to his execution as a heretic in Baghdad in 922CE. This talk led to an offer to teach a course at the University of Cairo. It would be an opportunity to teach in Arabic, the language that he loved. He always remembered that his first desperate prayer to God was expressed in Arabic. Now he had an opportunity to teach Arabic students with an approach to learning that would encourage them to go beyond the traditional teaching methods of memorization to which they were accustomed. Once again he put off his decision to join Foucauld in the Hoggar.

Returning to Cairo in 1912 Louis' silent vows to a religious vocation felt challenged. It became more and more difficult to avoid returning to his way of life before his conversion experience. He and Luis de Cuadra were invited to many evenings with socially prominent Europeans in Cairo. At the home of the Austrian consul and his wife, Countess Hohenwaert, Massignon met a 25 year old Egyptian woman of Syrian and German background. Her eminent Catholic family had immigrated to Egypt in 1775. Mary Kahil spoke fluent Arabic and was educated in Europe. After many evenings at the home of the Countess, Massignon spoke to Mary of his vow to offer himself in substitution for his friend Luis de Cuadra's return to Christianity. When Luis became seriously ill and almost died of Typhus, Massignon asked Mary to join him in his prayer of mystical substitution so that his friend would make his confession and give up Islam. Mary agreed to join in the prayer. Although Luis de Cuadra agreed to make a confession to a priest, he admitted when he recovered his health that he only did this to please his mother. Massignon was distraught. God seemed to reject his prayer.

Fearful that Mary was becoming too attached to him Louis decided not to see her again. Twenty years later he would fault himself for his "sinful misogyny," and renew their spiritual friendship. Together they would found an educational and spiritual organization in Cairo dedicated to Muslim Christian relations called the *Badaliya*, which means the Substitutes in Arabic.

Massignon was nearly 30 years old when he returned to France in 1913, still uncertain of his vocation. He knew in his heart that he was not going to join Foucauld at Tamanrasset. The priest had chosen to concentrate on the Berber dialect rather than Arabic and that was a decision that Massignon, spiritually and as a linguist, could not make.

On the other hand he had made a promise to his spiritual mentor and often found himself caught up in his longing for the desert. Meanwhile his family was pressuring him to consider marriage. His father particularly did not want him to become a priest and was fearful that his son might actually choose to live in Africa with the desert priest, Foucauld.

Louis knew that a vow of celibacy was exposing himself to impossible temptations and yet he was still caught up in his resistance to the idea of marriage. He took pride in his asceticism which was decidedly fraught with misogynist feelings. The question of Tamanrasset was strangely resolved in 1913 when Foucauld returned to Paris to seek the backing of Abbé Fontaine for his Association. He invited Massignon to assist him in his celebration of Mass at a Carmelite crypt in honor of his great uncle who was martyred in the Terror of 1794. "But there," wrote Massignon, "a strange sign from God passed between us like a sword."[56] While Louis was waiting for Foucauld another priest asked him to assist his Mass and Louis followed him without hesitation. This sign convinced Louis that he was not meant to go with Foucauld to the Hoggar. The desert priest accepted Louis' decision with his customary humility.

Louis' talent and early success as a scholar and linguist were surely signs leading him to choose an academic path, and he did make that choice in 1913. But he also continued to support Brother Charles in his efforts to establish his Association. By now Foucauld had named his Association the Union of Brothers and Sisters of the Sacred Heart. Louis made his decision to remain in the academic world in France at the age of thirty and felt his next decision would have to be about marriage. In the five years since his conversion experience he had consistently turned to prayer and his spiritual mentors in discerning his life choices. It was essential to Louis to listen intently to where he felt God was leading him. He often went on retreats to the tombs of Saints who were significant to him to pray. Louis chose to marry and spent the rest of his life listening in prayer and paying attention to the signs that pointed the way to God's will for him. He remained a passionate disciple of Christ with an unmistakable religious call.

Louis wrote to Père Foucauld about his decision to marry and also asked about becoming a member of the new Union. Brother Charles wrote back on September 30, 1913 that he was touched by Louis' desire to join the prayer Union of Brothers and Sisters of the Sacred Heart and would arrange it for him. He continued:

"With all my heart I pray for you that you are and do at every moment what Jesus wishes, in the plan to marry and in everything.... If God wishes you to marry don't accept it as expiation but as the state in which he has reserved the most graces for you, where you are able to glorify him the best, to sanctify yourself the most, to make His Reign in you and in others, to do His will, and help others to do so.

The state of marriage is not an expiation but a holy state which we enter through a sacrament by which we are able, and must, sanctify ourselves and others... To father children who have immortal souls destined to love and serve God eternally in heaven, is probably to be the author of a line of very happy souls who will adore God forever, how grand and what an admirable vocation!..."[57]

Louis Massignon was the 48th person to join Brother Charles' Union of Brothers and Sisters of the Sacred Heart. Despite Brother Charles' support for his decision to marry, Louis was acutely aware of the priest's disappointment that he would not join him in the desert and eventually succeed him in Tamanrasset. It seems that Louis would hold that sadness in his heart for the rest of his life. On January 27, 1914 Louis married his cousin, Marcell Dansaert-Testelin with Abbé Fontaine's blessing. Just previous to the wedding he delivered his manuscript to the Sorbonne for his principal thesis, "The Passion of al-Hallaj."

For their honeymoon Louis planned to visit Montserrat and then finally make his trip to the Sahara with his new wife so that Père Foucauld could bless their marriage in person. However, the desire for the hermit priest's blessing in person was never fulfilled. The trip to Tamanrasset was prevented by the head of the station when they reached Touggourt because the road was too dangerous. Instead they returned via Maison Sarrée where the Superior General of the White Fathers blessed their marriage on behalf of Charles de Foucauld.

Louis continued his correspondence with Brother Charles. His first son, Yves, was born on March 1, 1915. World War One had already begun. In October 1916 Louis wrote to the hermit priest of his decision to request to be sent into combat. For Brother Charles, still a soldier in his heart, devoted to both his country and his God, choosing the danger and hardship of combat was part of the sacrifice and devotion of a Christian.

His letter to encourage Louis' choice was written a few hours before his tragic death on December 1, 1916. He wrote, "If God preserves your life, which I ask Him to do with all my heart, your home will be all the more blessed because you sacrificed more, you will be more united to Jesus and have a more spiritual life. If you die, God will take care of Madame Massignon and your son, without you, as you would have taken care of them.... Have confidence that God will give you the destiny that glorifies Him the most...."[58]

Louis did not find out about Brother Charles' death until his wife sent a newspaper clipping. It arrived on his wedding anniversary, January 27, 1917. Brother Charles was not a martyr in the usual sense. He was not a soldier in combat, but a hermit priest who was meant to be taken hostage rather than shot accidently when the young man designated as his guard panicked. The joy in Brother Charles' letter at Louis' choice for danger and hardship suggested to Louis that he had somehow fulfilled the desires of the former officer. When he received this letter he was struck by Brother Charles' prayer that God preserve his life. He wrote, "By a strange exchange, he was killed and I was protected.... Beside myself, I climbed onto the parapet of the snow covered trench, seized by a feeling of sacred joy, and cried out, 'he found his way, he succeeded'!"[59]

Through many letters and three brief meetings with Père Foucauld, Louis Massignon recognized the extraordinary fire of love that burned in the heart of the hermit priest. The small Association had 49 members and when Brother Charles was killed they were afraid that it would not survive. On his return to Paris, Massignon suggested that René Bazin write the hermit priest's biography. He dedicated himself to promoting Pére Foucauld's vision of a prayer Association keeping it alive until the Fraternities began to be envisioned in 1932. It took 12 years, from 1917 to 1928, for Massignon to receive the permission from Rome to publish the priest's spiritual Directory which guided the continuation of the Association and eventually the establishment worldwide of the communities, known as Fraternities, of the Little Brothers and Sisters of the

Sacred Heart of Jesus. Throughout the early years of these communities Massignon remained a link to Père Foucauld's spiritual legacy and provided advice and direction for the brothers and sisters.

Louis Massignon was influenced by Brother Charles in many ways, both in his public life of research and teaching about Islam and the Muslim world and in his own spiritual life. "How many times since 1917 have I received visits from persons unknown to me sent by Foucauld…?"[60] In 1950 he once again felt called by Brother Charles when he was finally able to take his wife to Tamanrasset. On October 19th he spent the night in prayer at Père Foucauld's fort. "I had my night of adoration with Foucauld, in his *Borj*; dark night, darker than that first night of praying together at the Sacre Coeur in 1909; still poorer and reduced to ashes. But the Arab proverb says; God knows how to see the black ants crawling on the black stone in the dark night."[61]

Part Three: The Spiritual Legacy

There is no doubt that whatever actually occurred in Iraq in 1908, the young Louis Massignon had an experience of God that changed him forever. He openly referred to that experience in his letters and conversations but did not describe the experience publicly until much later in his life. In 1960 he quoted one of Brother Charles' Moroccan guides as saying that contact with Islam was the great experience in the hermit priest's life.[62] Massignon could well have been speaking of himself. By opening their hearts to the religion of Islam and their Muslim friends both men found their Christian faith renewed and enhanced. From 1906 to 1916 Louis Massignon received about 80 letters from Père Foucauld who he came to think of as an older brother.

The fundamental themes that permeated Massignon's spirituality were present from the very beginning of his conversion experience and continued to develop to the end of his life. He felt guided throughout his life by the spiritual intercession and example of Père Foucauld whose devotion in prayer, and unquestionable loyalty and respect for his Muslim hosts in Tamanrasset, nurtured his own understanding of his faith. At the very core of Christianity is an interconnected mystical experience that both men described as Substitution, Hospitality and Compassion. These are not abstract ideas but rather felt by hearts living intensely in relationship with others, both in joy and suffering, and transformed by an amazing experience of God's merciful love.

Conversion:

Both Charles de Foucauld and Louis Massignon had an experience in their mid-twenties of God breaking into their lives. Radically changed, both men struggled with what it meant to live out their new found faith in the context of their lives. In his conversational style of praying and writing to his God, Père Foucauld wrote:

> "Independent of my will, exterior events forced me to detach from material things which had a lot of appeal for me, and which held back my soul and attached it to the earth. You violently broke these ties like many others! How good You are, my God, to have shattered everything around me, to have so annihilated everything which prevented me from belonging to You alone..."[63]

In 1955 Louis Massignon responded to an inquiry about God with the following description of his conversion experience in 1908, in which he described the human soul personified as a woman, and his experience of God as the *Visitation of the Stranger*.

> "The Stranger who took me as I was, on the day of His wrath, inert in his hand like the gecko of the sands, little by little overturned all my acquired reflexes, my

precautions and deference to public opinion. By a reversal of values He transformed my relative ease as a propertied man into the misery of a pauper....Before the Lord who struck the blow, the soul becomes a woman....She starts only to commemorate in secret the Annunciation, viaticum of hope, that she has conceived in order to give birth to the immortal. This frail Guest that she carries in her womb determines thereafter all of her conduct. It is not a made-up idea that she develops as she pleases according to her nature, but a mysterious Stranger whom she adores and who guides her. She devotes herself to Him."[64]

The experience that we call conversion may begin, as it did for Louis Massignon, as a sudden awareness of God striking an internal blow that causes us to painfully face ourselves and the attachments in our lives. We open our hearts to the realization that we are not as good, kind, honest, or loving as we like to think of ourselves. In fact, we have been selfish, greedy, and pleasure-seeking. We feel judged by God with the same standards by which we have judged others. Now we see our actions and failed relationships for what they are. We finally begin to understand the meaning of the word "sin." As Père Foucauld suggests, our ties are violently broken with a world that tempts us to imagine our happiness can be bought by more and more high-tech products and luxuries. We are suddenly feeling asked to pay attention to something else.

In the poetic language that seems to be the only way words can capture such an overwhelming experience, both Père Foucauld and Louis Massignon write that our souls must not be held back by our attraction to the world and its abundant material distractions. We feel our poverty in the face of God's abundant life. At the same moment that we feel deep regret for our sinful behaviors and self-centered choices, miraculously we know without a doubt that we are forgiven, the debt has been paid by the One who died for us on a cross. We feel saved by God's mercy. The Stranger/God who enters into relationship with our human souls impregnates us with the divine Guest, shows us how much we are loved and encourages us to give birth to God's love in our world. Both Père Foucauld and Louis Massignon realized that they now belonged to God. It was this realization that radically changed how they experienced themselves and others and led to the themes of ongoing conversion that became the ground of their spiritual lives.

Substitution:

In his correspondence with Père Foucauld, and perhaps by his earlier exposure to J.-K. Huysmans and Saint Lydwine, the experience of continuing conversion seemed to lead Louis Massignon more deeply into the need to offer himself to God for others. Well before his conversion experience in 1908, he had already seen a connection between the saint and martyr of Islam, al-Hallaj, and the Christian Savior, the crucified Jesus. He was struck by one phrase by Hallaj found in Attar's *Memorial of the Saints*. The following translation of it reveals more of its meaning:

> "To lie prostrate twice [before God] is enough for the Prayer of desire; but the ablution [cleansing] that validates them must be made in blood."[65]

Five times a day faithful Muslims lie prostrate before God in their desire to submit themselves to the will of Allah. But Hallaj writes, that although this prayer is enough to demonstrate our desire to be authentically cleansed of all the sins that keep us from God, a price must be paid in blood. It took the words of Hallaj speaking to Muslims for Massignon to understand the sacrifice of the Christian Savior, Jesus, whose sweat was said to fall to the ground in drops of blood as he prayed to the God he called Father to take this cup from him. Yet, in the next breath he submitted himself completely to the will of his Father. The seed was sown for Massignon to understand Jesus' suffering on the cross and the shedding of his blood for the sin of humanity, as the first substitute in a long line of saints and mystics who followed.

In his daily notes on January 4, 1916 Père Foucauld wrote:

> "At the same time that he receives the name of Jesus, 'Savior', Our Lord sheds his blood, thus showing that it is through blood, through suffering offered to God, that one saves souls."[66]

Massignon and Foucauld both knew what it was to prostrate themselves before God. One month after his dramatic conversion experience, Louis Massignon wrote in his notes on June 24, 1908:

> "Suddenly, wrenching sensation of the presence of God, no longer judge, but father, inundating the prodigal son. I softly closed the door to my room with a key and stretched out on the tile floor, finally crying my prayer the whole night after five years with a dry heart."[67]

Until his death in 1962 Louis Massignon prayed the Stations of the Cross lying prostrate with his face against the ground. He told his son, Daniel that he did this in order to pray in solidarity with his Muslim friends.[68]

Massignon was greatly influenced by Père Foucauld in his understanding of the role of the Priest in consecrating the host for Communion as another sign of substitution, which fueled his own desire to become a priest himself. To imitate Christ clearly meant to sacrifice, to offer oneself for others. In a letter written to Massignon in 1910 Père Foucauld wrote:

> "Be of good courage, beloved brother in Jesus. Think often of the salvation of others; pray for souls, prepare to devote yourself to their salvation, to live for their salvation… To work for the salvation of souls is the life of anyone who understands Jesus, since it was Jesus'

own life. 'I give you a new commandment, that you love one another', and to love a person is to work for their salvation."[69]

All of his education prepared Charles de Foucauld for a career in the military and to adopt the French colonial views of his time. It was only his passionate experience of God in Jesus that allowed him to transcend such strong cultural influences and dedicate his life to loving others in this way. Nevertheless, he was not entirely successful in overcoming his military leanings and colonial views and influenced the young Massignon's own military choices. It took many more years and another World War for Massignon to act on his own experience of Jesus' commandment to love one another and fully resist French colonialism in Algeria.

The hermit priest hoped to the end that Louis would follow him by becoming a priest and take on his ministry in Tamanrasset. Even though Massignon made the decision to pursue his academic career and marry, he continued to struggle spiritually, pulled by his longing to somehow give his life to God and fulfill his mentor's wish for him. In some way both these men were drawn to extremes, as they needed to be in order to see the Muslim and Arab cultures as people worthy of God's saving grace rather than as heathens needing to be civilized and colonized by the French. Only God has the power to radically change our arrogant beliefs in national superiority and to bring us into authentic relationships with others grounded in love. Both Foucauld and Massignon were tempted by the forbidden and foreign and their passion to know the stranger. It led them both into the desert physically and spiritually and into unfamiliar languages and cultures.

Massignon tried to put aside his longing for the priesthood and accept his family as his priority. In Egypt, in 1934, he renewed his relationship with Mary Kahil and they founded a small prayer group at Damietta which they called the Badaliya, which means the Substitutes. It was dedicated to the mystery of the prayer of intercession and substitution. The heart of

Massignon's spiritual vocation was to pray for the Muslims and the Arab world. Like Foucauld he wanted to work for the salvation of souls. He finally fulfilled his desire to become a priest in 1950 when he received permission from Rome to become a priest in the Eastern Melkite Rite where married men were allowed to be priests. Once again Massignon was stretching the rules and reaching for the unusual. His decision was controversial even in Rome and only accepted with the understanding that he would not be an active priest in a parish but rather celebrate communion and his vow privately. His family also struggled to understand his great spiritual drive.

Massignon's passion and level of commitment to his faith experience are an invitation to us to stop and take stock of our own meagre efforts to live the spiritual life. For Foucauld and Massignon, mystical substitution was an inevitable result of understanding the life of Jesus. We are all called to work for the salvation of others by loving them as brothers and sisters. Although Massignon was not called to suffer and die for others as were so many medieval saints, Massignon's substitution was lived as a communion of friendship and love. For Massignon the sacrifice of the Mass is not only a sign of Christ's Passion but also a sign and symbol of shared love.[70]

In a letter written at Christmas in 1956 to members of the Badaliya Massignon wrote:

> "Meditate on the meaning and scope of our commitment, because if 'substitution' is before everything a thought, a vow of our souls, it is truly only accomplished if we take into our lives and our hearts of flesh the pain of others, their bleeding wounds, in nonviolence, through compassion and other's interior tears; then teach it to others."[71]

Seen in this light, our prayer for others' well being becomes an intense experience of allowing ourselves to feel their pain or difficulty as if it were our own. If we sincerely enter into this meditation we will inevitably be led to an extraordinary conclusion. By being able to cross over to another person's experience, we have the capacity to understand rather than dismiss, to forgive rather than condemn, and to make peace rather than war in our broken world. We would find ourselves meditating deeply on the meaning of compassion.

Compassion:

Massignon owed much of his understanding of his own vocation to Père Foucauld. He writes:

> "I feel obligated to explain to you how, through this living experience of the sacred in others, Foucauld was given to me like an older brother, and how he helped me to find my brothers in all other human beings, starting with the most abandoned ones... I needed him to communicate to me, through spiritual contact, in very simple words, by interviews and letters, his experiential initiation into the real understanding of the human condition, his experiential knowledge of the compassion which drew him to the most abandoned of human beings."[72]

In a letter to a friend in 1902 Père Foucauld wrote:

> "You know that to love is to forget oneself for another who we love a thousand times more than ourselves. To love is not to be concerned nor desire to be happy, but only to desire with all one's heart that the other be loved."[73]

From Tamanrasset on January 12, 1916 he wrote to Massignon:

> "In order to love God, practice loving people; in every human being see a child of God, a brother of Jesus for whom he died, a soul to save...In the sight of God,

nothing brings us to God's love better than charity towards His children."⁷⁴

Well before his own conversion experience, while still a child, Charles' cousin Marie showed him the statue of the Sacred Heart of Jesus that her family had donated to their church. This memory became the image of Jesus that travelled to the desert with him and speaks most deeply of Père Foucauld's spirituality. His letters to Massignon were signed, 'I love you in the Heart of Jesus." Massignon read and reread these letters from Père Foucauld throughout his life and found in them, as we do, a profound understanding of God and the human condition. Brother Charles' experience of God as Love, like that of Thérèse of Lisieux, went beyond the Church of his time, which most often presented God in terms of Divine Justice. But Père Foucauld's experience of his God led him to say that if we truly love God, we will also love our brothers and sisters. If we want to know how to love God we begin by loving other human beings.

It is crystal clear that Père Foucauld knew how hard it is to truly feel love in our hearts and to resist the temptations in our lives. He was not immune to temptations of his own, to dry periods in prayer, and the feelings of intense personal poverty of spirit. Even on the day of his death on December 16, 1916 Père Foucauld wrote to his sister from Tamanrasset:

> "We feel that we suffer, we don't always feel that we love, and that is the cause of even more suffering, but we know that we would like to love, and to desire to love is to love."⁷⁵

An intense personality like the young Louis Massignon found himself struggling with self-condemnation and wrote to Père Foucauld of the suffering he experienced. The hermit priest replied in a letter to Massignon written on August 1, 1916:

"I believe there are no words of the Gospel that have made a more profound impression on me and transformed my life than these, 'All that you do to one of these little ones you do to me'. It is perhaps in the leaving of yourself in order to go with all your energy to Jesus in others that God has put the best remedy against your temptations; temptations permitted by God in order to give you humility, defiance of self, consciousness of our profound poverty, and indulgence and pity for the other of which we have such a great need."[76]

Perhaps it is only these experiences of our own failings and need for a merciful and loving God that allows us to be compassionate to other human beings. It is only when we struggle with the reality of our own human condition and vulnerability that we can meet one another with the compassion that God has already shown to us. Louis Massignon learned that there is a value in suffering if it leads to compassion for others. On July 16, 1916 Père Foucauld wrote to Massignon:

"If it happens that we succumb to temptation, it is that our love is too weak, it is not that it does not exist; it is necessary to cry like Saint Peter, to repent like him, and be humiliated like him, but also to say three times like him, 'I love you, I love you, you know that despite my weaknesses and my sins, I love you....' As for the love that Jesus has for us, he has proved it enough so that we believe it without feeling it... Tell yourself often two stories, the graces that God has done for you personally since your birth, and the stories of your infidelities. We will find in them, especially we who have lived far from God a long time, the most certain proofs of His most attentive love for us, as well as, alas, the numerous proofs of our poverty..... He loves us because He is good, not because we are..."[77]

Hospitality:

It was to the hospitality shown to him by the Muslim Alussy family that Massignon sincerely felt he owed his life. And it was in their midst that he had his extraordinary experience of the presence of God. This was a Muslim family who welcomed him into their community, protected and aided him in achieving his archeological mission, prayed for him when he was hospitalized, and insured his safe journey home. They were his hosts in an Arab country on the verge of a revolution, who at great personal risk, welcomed and cared for a stranger. For the young Louis Massignon to find Christ in the midst of this Muslim hospitality was an overwhelming experience. His relationship with Père Foucauld enlarged his understanding of hospitality and it became a central theme in his spiritual life.

When at last Brother Charles made the decision to become a priest in order to live out his vision of the hidden life of Jesus in Nazareth, he wrote to Henry de Castries, on August 14, 1901, that he would continue his life in the Sahara, "not in order to preach, but to live the humble work of Jesus in solitude and poverty, trying to do good for souls. Not by speaking words, but through prayer, offering the sacrifice of the Mass, seeking forgiveness, and practicing charity…"[78]

Massignon wrote:

> "Foucauld was not constituted to vocally evangelize by propagandistic sermons. A messenger in our perverse times in which every expression is corrupted by technology, he came to share the humble life of the most humble, earning his daily bread with them by the 'holy work of his hands,' before revealing to them, by his silent example, the real bread of spiritual hospitality, that the humble people themselves had offered him, the word of Truth, the bread of angels, in the sacrament of the present moment."[79]

The sacrament of the present moment, a shared meal,

listening to a friend, helping another when we can, praying for one another, working together, is the hospitality that Père Foucauld and Louis Massignon came to understand as a spiritual reality. Louis Massignon was passionately interested in people and their stories. His spiritual legacy was lived out through concrete actions all the way to the end of his life. Volunteering to teach in the prisons and marching in the streets of Paris in resistance to French colonialism in Algiers, were the actions of a man who believed with his whole heart that human beings are all worthy of God's hospitality. Both he and Père Foucauld were compelled by the love and compassion they received from their God to offer that same gift of sacred hospitality to others. Père Foucauld once spoke to a Protestant Doctor who visited him in the Sahara:

> "I am not here to convert the Touareg at one go, but to try to understand them.... I am sure that the good God will accept into heaven those who are good and virtuous, whether they are Roman Catholics or not. You are Protestant, Teissière is a nonbeliever, the Touareg are Muslims. I am convinced that God will accept us all."[80]

In making this statement Père Foucauld had gone well beyond the church of his time. He had crossed over to the true meaning of hospitality, just as Louis Massignon transcended his culture by embracing his Muslim friends as brothers and sisters, and resisting the French colonial views of his time. But their understanding of hospitality was rooted in an experience of God, offered in daily communion as a nourishment for the human soul, and an intense experience of the meaning of the priesthood.

Massignon wrote:

> "Foucauld made me understand by his life, and especially by his death, that the priest is a vessel, an

alm of eternal hospitality, which has been passed on to him by a condemnation to die at the moment of being betrayed, delivered, executed."[81]

Massignon saw that Charles de Foucauld had been betrayed and executed, like Jesus. And, like Jesus, his death was his deliverance and his means of fulfilling his mission in the Sahara. Massignon himself was dedicated to the establishment of his friend and mentor's vision of the Little Brothers and Sisters of the Sacred Heart of Jesus. And he sincerely felt the presence of Père Foucauld interceding in his life and continuing to offer him eternal hospitality. He had been taught how to be Christ for others from an older brother through the experience of substitution, compassion and hospitality.

On April 19, 1911 Foucauld wrote:

"The more and more your heart enlarges, the more and more you will love, not only God alone, but first God and then all his creatures for Him…the more and more you feel the need to imitate the Beloved only in order to be made one with Him, the more you will love like Him, be one heart with Him, 'It is no longer I who lives, it is Jesus—the Heart of Jesus—who lives in me'."[82]

Chapter Three

Voicing the Inexpressible
Saint Thérèse of Lisieux and al-Hallaj

LOUIS MASSIGNON'S decision to write his dissertation on al-Hallaj had brought him to Baghdad and not only led to his conversion experience and lifetime spiritual journey, but also to 50 years of research on the life and spiritual legacy of the Muslim saint. Right from the beginning his experience of God seemed to lead him through Islam to Christianity and ultimately into a lifelong exploration and passion for both.

In 1908 after his unusual conversion experience in Baghdad, Louis Massignon returned to France accompanied by the Carmelite priest, Père Anastase-Marie de Saint Elie. In France, he continued to seek guidance from Père Anastase and it was he who suggested that Louis read *The Story of a Soul*, by Thérèse of Lisieux. The autobiography by the young French Carmelite nun was published the year after her death. At first Massignon was unimpressed but in November 1909 he mentioned in a letter to Paul Claudel that he was praying for her canonization. In 1911 in another letter to Paul Claudel he wrote:

"I believe that I owe a lot, during this very difficult week, to a Carmelite Saint from Lisieux, Sister Thérèse of the Child Jesus and the Holy Face, who died in 1897. From the end of 1908 I was asked to pray for the introduction of her cause for beatification in Rome and I resolved to force myself to do it without much taste for it, and to read her writings, which were sure to be devoid of anything literary! This little sacrifice, which is in fact within reach of intellectuals, permitted me to find vigorous consolations by reading her 'Life.' Do you know it? It is as humble as possible in story and style, yet great insight comes through it, ... which shows that holiness makes light of all obstacles,......."[1]

Part One: Two Lives

On April 9, 1888, at the age of fifteen, Thérèse Martin quietly dedicated her life to her God by entering the Carmelite Monastery in Lisieux, France. She chose the religious name Thérèse of the Child Jesus and the Holy Face. These were images that had profound meaning to Thérèse as she came to experience the life-giving presence of her God in both the birth of the child and the agony of self-sacrifice on the face of the crucified Jesus. On September 7, 1896 Thérèse began a private retreat which was to be her last before her untimely death at the age of twenty-four on September 30, 1897. When she was about to begin this final retreat her sister and godmother, who entered Carmel as Marie of the Sacred Heart, wrote Thérèse a note asking her youngest sister to write down her experience of prayer. Thérèse wrote:

> "I am going to stammer some words, even though I feel that it is impossible for the human tongue to express things which the human heart can hardly understand..."[2]

In 1898, one year following her death, the first printing of her autobiography, *The Story of a Soul*, which includes the writings from her final retreat, brought Thérèse of Lisieux out of the obscurity of a small community of cloistered nuns and into the minds and hearts of millions of readers worldwide. She was canonized as a Saint by the Roman Catholic Church on May 17, 1925 and on October 19, 1997 she became the third woman in history to be honored as a Doctor of the

Church. Because she lived in the late nineteenth century and her four cloistered siblings lived well into the twentieth century, today we can visit the house where she was born in Alençon and her family's home in Lisieux, or see the many personal articles on display at the Carmelite Monastery. We know what she looked like as a child and as a young woman from her photographs.

In contrast, the tenth century mystic/martyr of Islam known as al-Hallaj remains largely hidden to us in such a visually concrete way. Primarily due to a lifetime of meticulous research and documentation by Louis Massignon, we do have the still extant poetry and prose sayings, eyewitness accounts of his life and teachings, and a legend full of folk songs and poetic re-tellings of his passionate story of love and suffering. These remain a source of inspiration for the seeker of God and the spiritual life today. We know that Hallaj was Persian by birth and that he died a cruel death at the age of sixty-four by dismemberment and crucifixion. He was accused of being a heretic by the religious/political authorities of his time. He was a mendicant preacher who gained a considerable following of disciples in his travels throughout Iraq, Iran and as far away as India. He soon became known as a "reader of the inner secrets of the human heart."

Thérèse was born in 1873 in the small town of Alençon in Normandy, France. She was the last of nine children, although only five girls survived. As the youngest, Thérèse was showered with attention and affection. She was born in a politically turbulent time as the French republic struggled to establish itself. There was some fear of another revolution and much political division, with Catholics hoping for a return of the monarchy. Nevertheless, Thérèse was sheltered by her extended family and the small parochial Catholic town where she experienced religion as daily devotion and practical caring for the poor and marginalized in the community. As a small child she wanted to "please Jesus" and played games of being a nun.[3]

When Thérèse was four and a half years old her mother died of breast cancer and her father moved them to Lisieux to be close to his family. From this house, called Les Buissonnets, Thérèse watched each of her older sisters in turn leave home to enter religious life. The story of her childhood as she tells it herself draws us into the experience of her many losses which surely contributed to her developing understanding of her own call to a spiritual path. She tells us of her very early experiences of the Divine in her life and of her fascination with heroines such as Joan of Arc. She felt that she too was destined to live a life of glory for God, that she would be a Saint, and that she would dedicate her life to saving souls. By the age of fourteen she felt a great desire to start her religious life by entering the Carmelite Monastery at Lisieux.

That Thérèse grew up in such a sheltered environment and was inevitably educated in the traditional doctrine of the Church of her time, made the story of her life in Carmel even more remarkable. There she struggled to find her gift, her unique vocation. Her hidden desires were to passionately do heroic deeds for Jesus. She wanted to be a warrior, a martyr, a crusader, even a Priest. All vocations appealed to her.[4] Through her prayer and reflection she came to realize that they were all contained in one. Her vocation would be Love. At a time when the Church emphasized God as Justice, Thérèse envisioned God as Merciful Love. She writes, "All our justice is stained in Your eyes."[5] Despite her developing wisdom and the depth of her love, Thérèse experienced a dryness in her prayer for the majority of her years at Carmel. On June 9, 1895 she was inspired to offer herself "as a sacrificial victim to Merciful Love."[6] Her prayer to suffer in order to save souls for God was answered beyond anything she could imagine. On April 3, 1896 she began her true martyrdom of love as she experienced the first signs of the tuberculosis that would claim her life a year and a half later. Her final conversations were recorded in the last six months of her life.

From Massignon, and more recently the 1995 publication by Herbert Mason in English entitled *Al-Hallaj*, we know that Husayn ibn Mansur was born in 858 CE in a small town called Tur in southwestern Iran. His parents were Persian and spoke

Arabic. His father was a *hallâj*, a woolcarder. The family moved to southern Iraq where Hallaj received a traditional religious education in a Hanbalite Koranic school. There he would have memorized the entire Koran and studied commentaries. We don't know much about his family life or what led him to seek out a deeper commitment to his Muslim heritage as a disciple of the mystic and Sunnite Koranic scholar, Sahl. We do know that he became a Sufi, thereby committing himself to a specific mystical religious path. He married in 877 and settled in the town of Basra in Iraq, becoming the father of three sons and a daughter. His in-laws were Shi'ite Muslims.

Hallaj was influenced by the Hellenistic culture in Basra where he learned of other religious traditions and was exposed to the heated issues of social injustice at the time. It was here that he felt the divisions within his own Muslim tradition that would inspire his later passionate desire for a unified Muslim community and that would ultimately lead to his own martyrdom. He became an ascetic, purifying his own heart in preparation for his spiritual vocation as a witness to the Truth of the Transcendent God of Islam. His path was defined by a youthful energy that rejected more traditional Sufi attitudes towards political engagement, and he branded any suggestions of prayerful patience as "quietism." He adamantly opposed all political "extremism and tyranny" and felt called to a "personal mission." This mission began as his preaching attracted a loyal following of disciples.

His father-in-law's disapproval along with his earlier disagreements with his Sufi masters caused him to return to Iran and to avoid further connection with the Sufis. He was comfortable in society and became known in wealthy circles where he attracted patrons for his mission. But he also made enemies by his preaching to the crowds in the marketplaces. One of his themes was the role of Jesus in Islam. Later he was imprisoned and expressed his desire for martyrdom which he envisioned as death by crucifixion. Although he was accused of lack of piety and even heresy he remained a devout Traditionalist Muslim to his final agony. The intensity of his inner experience of God was expressed most poignantly in his poetry where he struggles with love of a God who is at once unknown and unknowable and intimately personal. He preached of a state of spiritual love for God alone and called his God, "Beloved", "Friend" and "You." His greatest fault, according to the religious and political powers of his time, was that he revealed his inner experience of God unabashedly in his preaching in the marketplaces. He was often found in states of ecstasy and seen by some as mad, a true fool for God. He spent his last nine years in prison in Baghdad and was finally condemned as a heretic. Future generations of Islamic communities continued to tell his story and his legend became known throughout the Islamic world. His passionate love of God is referred to in the poems of Islamic poets such as the well known mystic, Rumi. His story continues to reflect the controversy that arose around him and his message, but also claims his place as one of the world's greatest love mystics.

Part Two: Voicing the Inexpressible

Thérèse and Hallaj have two very different life stories and yet they fill our minds and hearts with images of love and longing for God that is a call to all of us. I believe that we cannot study the lives of the saints without being deeply affected by their efforts to express their experiences of the Divine. I have been changed by my own efforts to translate Massignon's Hallajian sayings from French into English. Visiting Alençon and Lisieux I followed the way of millions of pilgrims attracted to the places where Thérèse lived her short life. Despite the crowds of tourists and the immensity of a Basilica erected in her honor that Thérèse herself could never imagine, I was struck by the numbers of plaques lining the walls expressing thanksgiving to this holy woman for prayers answered.

Here are these two exceptional lovers of God brought together in a dialogue of their images of life and death in the Divine. I offer it in the spirit of Louis Massignon, whose spiritual life was nourished by both these exceptional mystics.

He came to respect and love Islam and his Arab and Muslim friends by "crossing over" to meet them and spent most of his life promoting interreligious understanding between Muslims and Christians and encouraging compassionate dialogue between the French and Arab peoples.

The Heart

Just as we struggle with understanding feelings of love for one another, and most often speak of love as felt in the heart, so Thérèse and Hallaj identify their own hearts as receptacles of Divine Love. Even more poignant is the mysterious experience they describe of a center point deep within the heart of the human soul that belongs to God alone. Hallaj calls it "*le point vierge,*" or the Virgin Heart. He wrote:

> "You live there, in my heart, where Your secrets reside. You are welcome to live there..... Because inside my heart nothing is more than You, there I recognize the supreme secret."[7]

> ".....virgin consciousness keeps itself for the Divine Secret in the intimacy of discreet hearts. And for their existence, at the core of their being, resides Existence Itself, The One Who claimed my heart, advising it and choosing it."[8]

In the last three months of her life others were to record carefully Thérèse's last words:

> "My heart is filled with God's will, and when someone pours something on it, this doesn't penetrate its interior; it's a nothing which glides off easily, just like oil which can't mix with water. I remain always at profound peace in the depth of my heart; nothing can disturb it."[9]

I imagine what it would mean if in my overwhelmingly secular world more and more people were to come to realize this secret. Hallaj and Thérèse suggest to me that the glimmer, or sometimes passionate love we feel in our hearts is only a tiny reflection of the Source of all love that resides in the depth of every human soul. My part is to welcome that Divine presence and to know that nothing can disturb it. "Nothing" feels like such a big word. When I am frantically trying to get too many things done in one day, feeling harried by the congested traffic on the way to work, feeling hurt by my coworker, or angry at my spouse, nothing can disturb that Virgin Secret. Could that knowledge change my heart? Would it melt my anger and daily frustrations and turn them into calm and compassion? Would I see my colleagues and friends differently if I knew that they too have this untouchable pure light of the Divine within them? And what if more and more of us saw every human being, every marginalized person, every stranger, every person of a different race or nationality, as a secret, sacred home for the Divine?

Nothingness

Thérèse speaks of her spiritual path as her "little way." She explains it this way:

> "It is to recognize our nothingness, to expect everything from God as a little child expects everything from its father; it is to be disquieted about nothing, and not be set on gaining our living….I was incapable of making my living, which is the eternal life of heaven…. To be little is not attributing to oneself the virtues that one practices, believing oneself capable of anything, but to recognize that God places this treasure in the hands of His little child to be used when necessary; but it remains always God's treasure. Finally, it is not to become discouraged over one's faults, for children fall often, but they are too little to hurt themselves very much."[10]

Hallaj wrote:

"....the saint who is stripped of everything, whose essence has become simple obedience, poor and naked, knows very well that it is God who does everything in him, that there is nothing other in him, and that he exists only through his Beloved, Who is truly his All."[11]

Thérèse and Hallaj are contradicting everything that I have learned in my culture that preaches psychological health as my personal accomplishment, and that my reward is money and recognition. I have arrogantly bought into the individualism that claims my egotistical right to have material things, and the illusion that my talent and ability belong to me. I am profoundly challenged by this 10th century Muslim who suggests a greater truth and by a twenty-four year old child-Saint who raises "littleness" and "childlike" from pejorative terms to the height of spiritual wisdom. What would happen if I "knew" in the depth of my heart that I am nothing, that everything that I am and can accomplish, my life itself, is a gift from a benevolent God? I feel a softening of my hardened heart, a weakening of my strident stance, a gentle push towards feeling grateful rather than proud, humble rather than arrogant. Who am I in my nakedness, stripped of all the illusions of my own powers, and placed instead in the hands of God? Who, if not a child, innocent and open to the wonder of life and free to take in every detail as a treasure? What a relief to know that I am incapable of "earning" the eternal life of heaven, that I will sometimes fail and have embarrassing faults, and that all of it is God's own treasure.

Suffering

Thérèse describes a passage from the Bible known as the Suffering Servant as inspiration for her devotion to the Holy Face:

"'Who has believed our report? Who could have seen the Lord's hand in this? It was the will of the Lord that his servant grow like a plant taking root in dry ground. He had no dignity or beauty to make us take notice of him. There was nothing attractive about him, nothing that would draw us to him. We despised him and rejected him—we ignored him as if he were nothing.' These words of Isaiah[12] have made my whole devotion to the Holy Face, or, to express it better, the foundation of all my piety. I too have desired to be without beauty, alone in treading the winepress, unknown to everyone."[13]

In a poem dedicated to Joan of Arc, Thérèse wrote:

"Ah! If the God of Love in this valley of tears
 Had not come to seek betrayal and death,
 Suffering would hold no attraction for us.
 Now we love it, it is our treasure."[14]

Hallaj wrote:

 "O, people! When God seizes a heart, He empties it of all that is not Him. When He attaches Himself to a person He doesn't let him live for anything but Himself. When He takes in affection one of His faithful, He incites the others to persecute him so that His servant searches for Him and comes closer to Him."[15]

The physical pain and emotional suffering that I have experienced in my life has forced me to search deeply for some sense of meaning. It is even more difficult to look beyond my personal experience to a world filled with clearly senseless suffering. In fact, it is perhaps too great a subject to tackle, and yet both Thérèse and Hallaj invite me to look at it once again. It is perhaps the most authentic place where God is present. We have no tolerance for suffering in our society and little acceptance of those who are not beautiful. There is a pejorative connotation to the word servant.

We expect modern medicine to take away our physical pain with pills and there are more and more psychotropic medications to relieve our emotional pain as well. We idolize the current Hollywood images of beauty and find ourselves feeling undesirable if we don't have the "right" features, hair color or weight. We don't consider the poverty of our inner cities and rural areas, or refugees of war-torn countries, as connected to our personal lives. Our servants are low-paid employees who have no status in our culture. In each instance we are denying a larger reality.

Like the prophets before her, Thérèse turns the images upside down. She does not desire to be seen as beautiful. In fact she does not want to be known by anyone except her God. Her image of the servant is the one who is the closest to God. And that one, to her, is the image of the Holy Face of Jesus, rejected, suffering and dying, not for nothing but rather for everything. It is very much like the image of Jesus washing the feet of his disciples, explaining how we are to do this for one another. This image is of God serving us.

In her poem to Joan of Arc, Thérèse identifies her own suffering with that of her childhood heroine, revealing her understanding of it. This experience of God seems to me to be the most difficult to capture in words. For Thérèse, the image of God's suffering is the ultimate expression of compassionate love for her, and for all of us. She treasures her own suffering because she experiences suffering as the very image of the God she so loves. I once had an experience of extreme physical pain that caused me to cry out to God over and over again. In the midst of it I had an experience of knowing somehow that God too was experiencing my pain, not beside me, but somewhere within me. It didn't take away my suffering but it did take away my fear. Perhaps that experience captures something of what Thérèse is telling us.

Hallaj tells us that when we are called into relationship with God we won't want to live for beautiful things, or care much about our physical attributes. We may be misunderstood or even persecuted by others. And this will only increase our longing for the hidden God.

Suffering by itself is certainly senseless, yet both of these holy people saw God intrinsically connected to it as a path to life, a symbol of love, a sign of holiness. Certainly not to seek it out, but to accept it when it comes knowing that Merciful Love is present in the agony of the Holy Face and will lead us to new life. It is our holy faces that cry out to God in our agonies, and it is the Virgin Heart in the soul of each of us who answers.

Unity

On May 8, 1884, at the age of eleven, Thérèse received her First Communion. She wrote:

> "For a long time now Jesus and poor little Thérèse looked at and understood each other. That day it was no longer simply a look, it was a fusion; they were no longer two. Thérèse had vanished as a drop of water is lost in the immensity of the ocean.... She felt so feeble and fragile that she wanted to be united forever to the Divine Strength!"[16]

Eleven years later she was inspired to offer herself to Merciful Love:

> "I beg You, O my God, to be Yourself my Sanctity."[17]

Thinking of the words spoken by a Mme. Swetchine, she felt "on fire":

> "Resignation is still distant from God's will; there is the same difference between the two as there is between union and unity. In union there are still two; in unity there is only one."[18]

Hallaj wrote:

"And where is Your face? Must my sight look for it in the intimacy of my heart, or in the pupil of my eye?"[19]

"I have become the One who I love, and the One I love has become me! We are two spirits merged into one body! To see me is to see Him and to see Him is to see Us."[20]

"He is closer than consciousness is for the imagination, and more intimate than the sparks of inspiration."[21]

Perhaps it is only with the innocence and sensitivity of a child that we can allow ourselves to feel so at one with God, and yet, Thérèse and Hallaj both grow ever more secure in their conviction that all that is holy within them is of God. For Hallaj, to lose himself in God becomes his sole desire. When Thérèse declares her vocation to be Love she understood that every vocation is Divine Love expressing itself in the world through us. I cannot remain unaffected when I finally grasp some sense of what they are experiencing. What Hallaj calls the Virgin Heart is the Divine spark in every human soul that not only calls me to be one with God but insists that I already am. What's more it is this bond of Love that ties me to every person on earth. Striving for unity in God is far more than a personal desire. It is an increasing recognition that the more I experience of God the more I will be able to love those around me.

Holiness is a word we hardly dare use in our culture. It evokes images of something inaccessible and too perfect for me to apply to myself or to others. And yet Thérèse and Hallaj describe it in terms of love and a profound desire for union with it. I cannot do my work as a psychotherapist unless I do it lovingly. We cannot share life together with another person unless we do it lovingly. I can only catch a glimmer of the oneness in God that they experienced but they call me to desire it; to imagine what it would be to see as God sees, to speak knowing that it is no longer I, but God who forms my words. The miracle that I have begun to recognize in reflecting on the writings and spoken words of this Christian Saint and Islamic Martyr is that, although they were one thousand years apart in time and come from two distinct religious traditions, they both lead us to the reality of God as Love. Love is surely holiness, with our flaws and weaknesses and fears an intrinsic part of the story.

Absence

Writing to her sister Pauline, Mother Agnes, who was Prioress of Carmel at the time, Thérèse wrote:

> "I should have written to you about the retreat preceding my Profession… it was far from bringing me any consolations since the most absolute aridity and almost total abandonment were my lot. Jesus was sleeping as usual in my little boat."[22]

She sang:

> "My heaven is to smile at this God I adore when He is hiding and testing my love."[23]

At a time when Thérèse felt "a living and clear faith" she could hardly believe that there were those who had no faith. It was then that she experienced a trial of her own. She wrote:

> "[Jesus] permitted my soul to be invaded by the thickest darkness, and that the thought of heaven, up until then so sweet to me, be no longer anything but the cause of struggle and torment. This trial was to last not a few days or a few weeks, it was not to be extinguished until the hour set by God Himself and this hour has not yet come."[24]

Like Thérèse, Hallaj too experienced God as absent. He wrote:

"I tried to have patience, but can my heart be patient deprived of its center? Your Spirit little by little mixes with my spirit making alternate comings and goings."[25]

"What importance now if the night of abandonment falls slowly or quickly, if it is truly Him, my Friend. What hope, that the night of abandonment watches with remembrance !"[26]

"Your image is in my eye, Your memorial on my lips, Your life in my heart, but where do You yet hide?"[27]

"Creatures wander in a shadowy night while searching for You, and only perceive allusions. It is by conjecture and imagination that they find their way towards God, and, turned toward the atmosphere, they call out to the heavens. Now, God is among them in every event, in all their states, from hour to hour. They would not withdraw from Him for a wink of an eye if they knew! Because He does not withdraw from them, no, not at any moment!"[28]

It is not as hard for me as it was for Thérèse to imagine a world filled with people who have no faith experience at all. The foundation of Democracy in my culture is the separation of Church and State which is an effort to maintain the religious freedom that brought so many to a new world. It has encouraged the establishment of many groups expressing diverse religious beliefs. It also respects the right of people to choose not to have religion in their lives at all. As a result, most of us spend a large part of our daily lives in secular environments where spirituality and religion are expected to remain a private concern. With little emphasis on religious values in our daily experience many have chosen to disregard it altogether. For others it has become a source of feeling alienated and unconnected to community and a larger meaning in life. The current rise of interest in spirituality in our culture is a reflection of that sense of loss.

Thérèse describes a crisis of faith that seems to be a necessary experience for those of us who do consider ourselves to be on a spiritual path. It is a time of doubt and insecurity and causes us to struggle with both our own spiritual experiences and our heretofore unquestioned beliefs. Thérèse believed she had to experience this confusion herself and described it as a "painful trial", a "dark tunnel", and the "night of nothingness." She came to understand it as increasing her desire for the "Light of heaven" that was so opposite to this dark tunnel, and ultimately it deepened her faith. It is the irony of the faith experience that insists that it is a kind of knowing in our hearts, or the core of our beings, that recognizes something is true without feeling anything, or seeing any concrete evidence of it.

Hallaj suggests that not seeing allows us to truly "see", and that even remembering in words, images, or prayers reminds us that God is hidden from us. God must remain hidden from us so that we will be wrenched from our complacency and driven by the longing that draws us closer and closer to Love. Lest we imagine that choosing to enter religious life in a monastery, or becoming an ascetic preacher is an easy path, Thérèse and Hallaj make it clear that experiencing God's absence is a painful yet essential component of faith and a part of the spiritual quest.

Hallaj gives me the most hopeful image when he reminds me that although my experience of God's absence feels like the shadowy night, God has not withdrawn from me. The Virgin Heart, that infinitesimal Light of God remains like Thérèse's Jesus, sleeping as usual in her little boat. As a person of faith, the dryness I experience in prayer, and the sometimes alienated feelings, serve to move me to a deeper interior level as my desire for God increases.

Even more poignant is Hallaj's suggestion that God is in every event, in every state of human experience. The hidden God is there from hour to hour in everyone. Even in those colleagues and friends, and members of my own family who choose not to acknowledge God, or have lost their family traditions, or those who were never introduced to religious practice at all.

Hallaj insists that God does not withdraw from those who are the most secular, materialistic, or politically ambitious and self-absorbed, even for a minute. What if those with no faith became aware that God will never abandon them? Would they still turn away? Would they find themselves, as Hallaj suggests, not wanting to lose that vision even for a wink of an eye?

Thérèse came to understand her dark night and live with it by experiencing it as God purifying her for the sake of all those who have no faith. This experience intensified her belief that her prayer and her spiritual experiences were of great benefit to others and the world. It was a remarkable belief that developed into a profound spirituality.

Dying for Love

At age 14 Thérèse wanted to dedicate her life to saving the souls of others. She imagined that she would do this by praying for them and by suffering for them. Her opportunity to try out her belief in the power of prayer came when she heard of a dangerous criminal who was to be executed and was known to be impenitent. She wanted to have the courage to pray for sinners and decided that she would pray for this man's soul. When she read in the newspaper that he did in fact repent at the very last moment she had her sign that her prayers had been answered.[29]

Thérèse offered herself as a substitute for others, when she recognized that her experience of darkness, of not experiencing heaven on earth, would allow her to offer her suffering for all those who live in darkness. For Thérèse those are the impious, people who do not recognize God. God will receive them into heaven if she puts herself with her whole heart, her love, between them and God.[30] She tells Jesus:

"I am happy not to enjoy this beautiful heaven on earth

so that He will open it for all eternity to poor unbelievers."[31]

She wrote that she knew that the Lord sent her this trial only when she was capable of bearing it. And that this state of darkness allowed her to have no other desire, even no desire for heaven, freeing her to desire only to love. On June 9, 1895 Thérèse wrote:

> "....It seems to me now that nothing could prevent me from flying away, for I no longer have any great desires except that of loving to the point of dying of love."[32]

Thérèse was convinced that her mission would never be understood except in the light of her sufferings. Then only could she be a source of inspiration and strength."[33] In the last stages of tuberculosis and suffering terribly Thérèse said:

> "Our Lord died on the cross in agony, and yet this is the most beautiful death of love.... To die of love is not to die in transports. I tell you frankly, it seems to me that this is what I am experiencing."[34]

> "Oh, how happy I will be, if when going to purgatory I can deliver other souls, suffering in their place, for then I would be doing good, I would be delivering captives."[35]

A few hours before her death she said:

> "No, I could never have believed it possible to have suffered so much! Never! Never! I can explain it only by the ardent desires I had to save souls."[36]

Just as mystical substitution became the heart of Massignon's spirituality so Thérèse clearly gave her suffering the same meaning.

The testimony given by a witness at Hallaj's execution describes his last vigil and "spiritual Testament." In his beautiful play, *The Death of al-Hallaj*, Herbert Mason brings Hallaj's last words to life. Hallaj prays through the night before his execution:

> "I cry to You, not only for myself
> But for those souls who yearn for You
> Whose witness, I myself, go now to You,
> the witness of Eternity"[37]

He was said to weep with laughter when he saw the gibbet where they were to crucify him. Asking for a prayer rug he recited:

> "Kill me, O my faithful friends
>   for to kill me is to make me live.
> My life is in my death, and my death is in my life."[38]

Massignon states that "Hallaj is the first Muslim mystic who desired to die out of sheer love."[39] He describes Hallaj's poems as the most "superhuman utterances of Islamic mysticism." He writes: "They are the fruits of a life liberated wholly through renunciation and sufferings, constantly renewed in God through prayer for the souls of others, and crowned by his passion for the unity of the Islamic community, carried as far as the desire (granted) to die condemned for its salvation."[40]

What kind of love is this that is so consuming that it compels these two spiritual giants to willingly die for it? We can hardly comprehend. And yet, they stand before us as witnesses to an experience of God's love that is so intense that it cannot be contained, spilling over to loving others, longing that we too become victims of Merciful Love. The stories of their suffering and dying have become an invitation for us to take seriously this God who loves us so passionately. We need these stories to inspire our own faith, to be witnesses for us of the power of Love to transform our world. It seems clear to me that Thérèse and Hallaj knew in the depth of their beings that their dying would bring God's message of love to new life in the world. And so it has for Muslims and Christians everywhere. Thérèse believed that she would "spend her heaven" saving souls on earth for Jesus through her love, causing them to love God as she did. Hallaj knew that his death would cause his message to spread throughout the Islamic world.

The Rose

The Heart of Christian/Islamic dialogue comes alive through the witness of passionate mystical lovers of God like Thérèse and Hallaj. This kind of love burns in the heart like a raging fire and lights the spark in us as we contemplate their efforts to voice the inexpressible.

While the crowd threw stones at the dying Hallaj, one was said to have thrown a rose. Massignon said that to throw a rose was an act of challenge. And so the legends of Hallaj's life and death began, and have become songs and plays and poems in which Hallaj is called "The Rose, the Red Rose."[41]

Mason's poem, *After Hallaj* ends:

"A blood rose may be thrown
by someone at your heart
An emblem of your now–
forgotten separation."[42]

Hallaj's last words were said to be the following:

"All that matters to the ecstatic is the increasing solitude of his Only One, in Himself."[43]

Playing in the garden at Alençon, flowers were a part of Thérèse's life from her earliest childhood. Later she participated in a Spring ritual every May of throwing petals at the large crucifix in the garden of the monastery in Lisieux. The image of the "unpetalled rose" became the subject of a poem in which

Thérèse describes herself as an unpetalled rose, the part of the flower that was thrown away after the petals were stripped from it. Like the unpetalled rose, she would abandon herself to her God. She wrote:

> "But the unpetalled rose is just flung out
> To blow away.
> An unpetalled rose gives itself unaffectedly
> To be no more.
> Like it, with joy I abandon myself to you,
> Little Jesus."[44]

On September 30, 1897, at seven in the evening, Thérèse died. Her last words were:

"Oh! I love You!"

Sister Agnes of Jesus wrote: "She had just lifted her eyes to heaven; what was she seeing?"[45]

Chapter Four

The Witness of A Saint
Saint Francis and The Journey to Islam

ALWAYS SEARCHING FOR links between Islam and Christianity, Louis Massignon spent many years contemplating becoming a Third Order Franciscan. Just as he found a spiritual mentor in Charles de Foucauld, who was often likened to Saint Francis in the way he lived his Christian call among the Berbers in Tamanrasset, he found support for his own experience of Islam in the Franciscan spirit.

By now Massignon was a well known Islamic scholar who had done years of research on the life and spirituality of al-Hallaj. His own spiritual journey seemed to lead him to Christian and Muslim saints and mystics, and to important biblical figures found in the Koran. Because Judaism, Christianity and Islam all claim Abraham as their patriarch he understood the great biblical figure as the link that binds them to one another. Abraham represented his own conversion experience and relationship with God. In his "Three Prayers of Abraham" he explores the themes of substitution, compassion and hospitality that were the ground of his own spirituality. These writings challenged the relationship of Christianity to other religions and ultimately influenced the Vatican II documents on interreligious dialogue and understanding in 1962.

Since his decision so many years before not to join his

mentor, Charles de Foucauld in the Sahara desert, Massignon continued to struggle with his intense religious calling. His success and extraordinary talent as a scholar, college professor, and diplomat could not be ignored, yet how was his relationship with his God meant to be lived in his daily life? There was a connection of Saint Francis to Islam that attracted Massignon to the saint. The way that Francis insisted that his brothers and sisters live the gospel message shaped his attitude towards the Muslims. The story of Saint Francis' visit to a Muslim sultan established the connection for Massignon and in 1931 he joined the Franciscan Third Order. When he made his final vows in 1932 he took the name of Abraham.

Details of Francis' life help us to understand the saint's spiritual journey and especially his approach to Islam, which was so different from the attitude in the religious culture of his time.

Part One: The Life of Saint Francis

> "If you will be perfect, go, sell what you have and give to the poor."
> "Take nothing for your journey."
> "If anyone wishes to come after Me, let him deny himself, and take up his cross, and follow Me."

These were the words from scripture that inspired the man who was known in Italy as the Poverello, "the little poor man," to say to his first three followers, "Here is what we are going to do, and all those who shall join us afterwards."[1] These words were spoken in the year 1208. Through the centuries the life of Saint Francis has become a legend and Franciscan communities of Brothers and Sisters are found in every country in the world. The legend describes Francis as a charismatic personality who joyfully embraced poverty and literally became a beggar out of his love for Christ.

Although the exact date of his birth is unknown, Francis was born in Italy at the end of 1181 or the beginning of 1182 into one of the wealthiest families in Assisi. His father, Peter Bernardone, was a cloth merchant but there seems to be little known about his mother, Pica, other than that she had two sons. Francis' brother was named Angelo. Apparently at Francis' baptism at San Rufino Church, Pica named him John, after John the Baptist. The confusion in relation to his name suggests that his father, who was in France at the time of his birth, renamed him Francesco on his return, perhaps in honor of his close business relationship with the French. On the other hand, it is quite possible that John was given the nickname Francesco when he became old enough to sing the songs that he loved by the French troubadours. This story serves as an example of the confusion surrounding the historical life of Saint Francis, and the difficulty in finding his life story after 800 years of legends and reported miracles.[2]

We do know that Francis had an elementary school education where he would have learned Latin, as well as reading and writing. However, he apparently did not write very well and later in his life dictated his letters and various documents related to the foundation of the Franciscan rule and community to one of his Brothers. The world that Francis knew at the end of the 12th century and into the 13th century was primarily Italy and regions of France that were dominated by Rome. But we also know that after some failed attempts to travel to Egypt he did succeed in 1219.

By the time Francis was born the social order in Italy was made up of large communes, having shifted from a rigid feudal system where people were born either into the nobility or as commoners. The nobility, called the "majores," were a hierarchy of dukes, counts, lords and knights who governed and kept order when there were uprisings, which were inevitable in a feudal society. The common people, known as "minores," were protected by their lords and knights and were divided into two groups. The "serfs" were considered a part of the Lord's property and belonged to him. The "villeins" were citizens and free men who worked as craftsmen, merchants or farm laborers and could also own property. But they were heavily taxed and because they were not nobility had no voice in the government. In this society the wealthy were the lords and their noblemen along with church officials and monastic communities.

The distribution of wealth shifted as a result of the crusades which opened up trade routes to the Byzantine Empire and allowed merchants and craftsmen to become very wealthy. They now bought and sold their goods throughout Europe, and through the fairs held in Provence and Champagne they had access to goods from Asia and Africa as well. Their wealth bought them a voice in the government and thus the possibility of gaining in status and becoming one of the majores. This new social order created a middle class of businessmen which benefitted a few villein but they often treated the serfs more harshly than their previous lords. Civil wars and family feuds ravaged Italy as the various communes struggled for power and property. This was the climate in the town of Assisi when Francis was born.

At the same time, glorious stories of knights in shining armor, like those of King Arthur's Round Table, spread from France to Italy with the songs of the wandering troubadours. These love songs and rhymes telling of gallant warriors, heroic knights saving their ladies from harm and vowing to protect the widows and orphans, contrasted dramatically with the corruption in the churches and the violence and extreme injustices shown the lower classes and enslaved serfs.

Although a commoner by birth and villein by trade, and extremely wealthy, Francis' father, Peter Bernardone, was not nobility. This may have been his hope for his son who might have gained in status by becoming a knight. In fact Francis was attracted to the heroic tales of chivalry and romance in the songs of the troubadours. He had a talent for singing and composed his own songs like the "jongleurs" who interpreted the songs of the troubadours into a local jargon.[3]

When Francis was still a young boy Pope Gregory VIII called for the third crusade to recapture Jerusalem from the Arab Muslim, Saladin. At the time, those Arabs who were followers of Mohammad were called Saracens. This crusade which lasted from 1189 to 1192 did not succeed. During his lifetime Francis would see both the 4th and 5th crusades to liberate the Holy Land.[4] In 1198 when Francis was 16 years old, the people of Assisi took advantage of a momentary absence of the representative of the Emperor, Duke Conrad of Urslingen, and rose up against the aristocracy. The citizens of Assisi wanted to create a free commune. Their success in extricating themselves from the power of the Emperor and also avoiding subservience to the Church caused a civil war with the neighboring city of Perugia where many of the aristocracy had fled. This struggle lasted 10 years.[5]

Francis worked in his father's business as a cloth merchant and likely travelled with him to France and to the fairs in other towns in Italy. According to his biographers, in his teens and early twenties Francis was popular and charming, easily mixing with both the sons of nobles and the middle class. The young people of Assisi entertained themselves with eating and drinking heavily at banquets and parading through the streets of Assisi singing and dancing. Inspired by the popular troubadours they serenaded young ladies and sometimes got into trouble with their revelry. Francis dressed extravagantly and clearly had a personality that attracted followers even in his youth. Apparently he lavishly spent his father's money on them as well. It isn't hard to imagine that Francis was full of vanity and the exuberance of youth, and like most young people, desired recognition and fame.[6] In 1202, at the age of 19, Francis joined in the battle of Collestrada against Perugia at Ponte San Giovanni and was taken prisoner for a year. His father was finally able to buy his release.

This year apparently affected his health so that on his return to Assisi Francis became ill and it took many months for him to recover. One day when he went for a walk in the country he was surprised to find that the sight of fields of wild flowers in bloom no longer lifted his spirits as it once did. It was a fleeting recognition of how our attachments, even to the beauty in nature, does not guarantee happiness. Perhaps this experience was a foreshadowing of the far greater changes that would affect

Francis' view of life later on. When he was fully recovered Francis once again set out to pursue his goal to become a knight. He joined a count from Assisi who was preparing to go to Apulia where the Pope's army was at war over the guardianship of the deceased Henry VI's heir to the throne.

Here his biographers suggest that Francis had a dream before leaving Assisi and possibly another on his way. Whether a dream or some sense of God's presence, something in Francis changed. He returned to Assisi where he waited to discover what was being asked of him. He began to pray, perhaps confiding in one close friend who accompanied him outside the city to a cave or solitary place where Francis prayed alone.[7] There he struggled with his youthful desires which he now experienced as sinful, yet there was something about his love for the honor, nobility and fidelity of the knights that sought expression. Tormented by doubts and conflicting desires Francis finally found his peace in God and emerged one day from his solitary prayer rejoicing.

Francis began to give away his money and his clothing to the poor and he once even exchanged his own clothing with that of a beggar. He was learning to deny himself in order to find his God. Francis himself reported his greatest test. In Francis' time, many unfortunate people were disfigured with the open wounds of leprosy. According to Francis he was repelled whenever he saw anyone with this terrible disease and found his disgust impossible to overcome. He said that God told him to go to these unfortunate people, and when he did so he found that what had seemed painfully beyond him became easy.[8]

Francis now knew that he wanted to live his life for God but his way was still unclear. Here the stories about him are conflicting but Francis did think that he was called to give away his money and tried to do so by offering to rebuild an ancient chapel that was built in 1103. His biographers write that one day in the year 1206 he went into this small chapel in the country not far from Assisi. The deserted chapel of San Damiano was old and left in ruins, being cared for by a lone priest who apparently lived there on the alms that were brought to him. Francis knelt to pray before the ancient wooden crucifix. They say that he heard the Lord calling him by name, "Francis, go repair my house, which is falling in ruins."[9] Looking around the decaying chapel Francis thought that his Lord was asking him to rebuild it. In one account he returned to Assisi and took the fabric that he was accustomed to selling in the markets to the town of Foligno. There he sold it and brought the money back to San Damiano. He tried to offer it to the priest for the restoration of the chapel but who would believe the "sudden conversion" of this well-known son of a wealthy merchant? The money was refused for fear of reprisals from Francis' father but the priest agreed to let him stay there.[10]

When Peter Bernardone heard what his son had done and where he was staying he went to find him. Francis hid from his family for a month eating very little and praying until he felt confident enough to face them. The formerly charming and flamboyant young man returned to Assisi, thin and worn out from his ordeal. Those who saw him were sure that he had lost his mind. His father dragged him home and tried to force his son to give up his religious ferver, locking him up so that he could not escape. When his father had to leave the house on business his mother, realizing that she too could not change his mind, freed him. Francis returned to San Damiano. Peter Bernardone's one last hope was to take away his son's inheritance and send him into exile. Perhaps that would cause Francis to think about his choices. He brought his son before the Bishop.

Bishop Guido II told Francis that if he truly wanted to follow Christ he would have to return his father's money and accept the loss of his inheritance. Apparently Francis immediately took off his clothes and returned them to his father as well. He then went for a few days to a monastery of monks where he hoped to earn some clothing by working in the kitchen but he was treated badly. From there he went on to the town of Gubbio where a friend gave him an inexpensive tunic to wear. Now he was dressed as a hermit and went to serve the lepers before returning to San Damiano.

Francis was now determined to rebuild the chapel. After his experience helping the lepers, who were certainly the poorest of outcasts in his time, Francis began to identify himself with the poor. He was determined to live as they did. In order to rebuild San Damiano he would have to beg for the stones and for his meals as well. Begging is certainly not easy for anyone, and was especially difficult for the son of a wealthy merchant. Perhaps this was how Francis began to experience humility. We are told that he sang through the streets of Assisi with songs of praise for God, inviting others to join him in rebuilding his church. Nevertheless, for all those who agreed to help him there were others who continued to make fun of him.

When the chapel of San Damiano was completed Francis still thought his mission was to rebuild churches. His biographers name San Pietro della Spina as one of them as well as an abandoned chapel deep in the woods in a valley below Assisi that once belonged to the Benedictine Abbey of Mount Subasio. Saint Mary of the Angels, known as the Porziuncola, became Francis' favorite and it was here that the Franciscan movement was born.

On February 24, 1208, Francis went to Mass in this newly renovated chapel. The readings from the Gospel of Matthew touched him deeply. Now he was certain of the path he would follow. "Go and preach the message, the kingdom of heaven is at hand…Freely you have received, freely give… Do not take gold, or silver, or copper for your belts, no sack for the journey, or a second tunic, or sandals or walking stick. The laborer deserves his keep. Whatever town or village you enter, look for a worthy person in it, and stay there until you leave. As you enter a house wish it peace."[11] Francis understood that he must trust in God alone to meet his needs. Now he knew that he was not being called to physically build churches but rather to build up the church with believers.[12] In the depth of his being Francis wanted to be like Jesus. He perceived both Jesus and his mother, Mary, as poor, therefore he too would be poor.

Francis was joined by three other young men who became his first brothers. His charm and his personal humility soon attracted others to his life of poverty and message of peace. Now there were eleven brothers. They begged from house to house for food and sang songs of God's love in the village square. In the beginning the people of Assisi thought they were mad. They either insulted them or ran away from them, resenting these young men who had given up their property and were reduced to begging for food at their doors. Francis thought of his young followers as disciples. He spent time teaching these men his vision of following Christ. If they were truly poor they would learn to trust entirely in God for their well being. He taught them to pray and to sincerely repent for their own sins, as well as to believe that they were bringing God's mercy to all those from whom they received alms. He taught them humility.

Francis took the Gospel message literally, sending his brothers out in pairs to different regions to invite the people to love God alone, repent of their sins, and live in peace with one another. Needless to say they were not always well received because of their ragged appearance. Yet the small band continued to attract followers. His biographers say that when their number reached 12, like the biblical 12 apostles of Christ, and they were once again gathered at the Porziuncola, Francis decided to formulate his first rule for their way of life and present it to Pope Innocent III for official approval. At this time the church was in dire need of reform. There were many people speaking out against the abuses and scandals. Heretical sects were forming in southern France and northern Italy. People were rising up against the church institutions. The Pope had good reason to be wary of this new group from Assisi.

Although the Bishop of Assisi initially thought that Francis' way of life was too difficult for the brothers to sustain he now supported Francis in Rome. Bishop Guido had begun to see the advantages of having this dedicated group in his region. He introduced Francis and his brothers to the Cardinal from San Paolo and it was Cardinal John who arranged their audience with the Pope. The Pope too had concerns about the future of a brotherhood which tried to live the Gospel message of poverty literally and yet it was clear to him that Francis' enthusiasm might promote true reform in the church. He gave his oral approval for the Rule of life for the Order of the Friars Minor. Francis' named his brothers after their calling to live as "minores" in the way of Christ and the apostles.[13]

From Rome the friars settled not far from the Porziuncola in a place called Rivo Torto where they lived in a small hut for many months. They sent a few out to beg for food each day and others did daily manual labor while they nurtured their calling with solitary prayer and fasting. It was during these months that the foundation for their spirituality was more solidly formed. Although Francis and his brothers were drawn to this life of solitude and prayer, Francis knew their vocation was to actively go out and teach, bringing others to Christ. Each weekend Francis went to Assisi where he gave a sermon in the Cathedral of San Rufino. When they were forced out of their hut in Rivo Torto the Abbot of the Benedictines of Mount Subasio offered Francis the chapel of Porziuncola and some land around it. To Francis this property was a loan that he and the friars would continue to pay for each year with their labor.

It is likely that a young woman named Clare di Offreduccio heard Francis preach at the Cathedral of San Rufino. She was from a noble family of "majores" in Assisi. Clare was about 11 years younger than Francis and was well educated, able to read Latin, and well versed in the popular and romantic stories of chivalry and the battles of the knights. At the age when her parents were arranging for her to marry Clare had other ideas. Clare was attracted to Francis' poetic sermons and songs and knew his story of leaving a wealthy family to embrace poverty out of love for God. But of course her family would not approve of her desire to join Francis' followers. Apparently Clare and Francis met secretly for many months and devised a plan for her to escape from her family. On Palm Sunday, March 18, 1212, she went to church with her family as was expected of her. That night when everyone was asleep she and one of her cousins left for the Porziuncola. There Francis met them and before the altar he cut off their hair and dressed them in the simple habit of the friars. He took them to a Benedictine monastery for women. Clare was 19 years old.

Her parents were unable to convince her to change her mind but when her 15 year old sister, Caterina, came to join Clare, Francis had to move them to another monastery at the foot of Mount Subasio to protect them from their father's anger. At that time the nuns were protected by a papal statement that prevented anyone from entering the nun's cloister. After some months, with the approval of Bishop Guido, the women were allowed to move to San Damiano. Clare and her Poor Ladies would live there until the end of her life. And it was only just before her death in 1253 that the Pope approved her Rule adopting a life of poverty in the spirit of the Friars Minor. Clare insisted that the sisters accept alms and not own any property. They would trust that God would provide for them. Now Francis had the powerful support of a cloistered praying community to complement the exhaustive travelling of the friars in their vocation to go out and teach the gospel throughout Italy and beyond.

Travelling in Italy and southern France with his message of peace and call to prayer and repentance, Francis began to attract more and more new friars. Some chose to live in hermitages and Francis established many in the mountains of Italy. He took a small group of brothers to one of them each year where they spent many months in solitude. While in Tuscany, about 100 miles north of Assisi, near San Marino, the Count of Orlando of Chiusi offered Francis a mountain called La Verna. There he established a hermitage which became an important place in his own spiritual journey near the end of his life.

The friars' numbers grew as many brothers from northern Italy and Tuscany began to join them. Like the legendary King Arthur who gathered his Knights of the Round Table once a year at Pentecost, Francis also began to call the friars to the Porziuncola during this Christian feast. Pentecost celebrates the promise of Christ to send the Holy Spirit into the minds and hearts of the disciples inspiring them to go out into the world to proclaim the good news of the Gospel. The gatherings at the Porziuncola came to be called General Chapters. They allowed Francis to meet the newest members of his growing community and to encourage them in their spiritual mission. Decisions were made to divide the brotherhood into provinces since their increasing numbers made it necessary to begin to form an organization, and to begin to send the brothers out to establish new missions in foreign countries.[14]

By the year 1219, when the friars came to the Porziuncola for their Chapter, they were no longer the small devoted group of brothers that gathered around Francis at Rivo Torto. Most of the brothers had never met him and there were many clerics who had their own ideas of what the Order should become. They wanted to be more like the other religious orders and were fearful of the persecution many of the brothers had experienced in their missionary efforts in foreign countries. They wanted more security and less poverty. For Francis following Christ meant embracing poverty and accepting persecution, and even crucifixion, with joy. Simplicity and humility were the foundations of his Rule and he knew that his way of living the religious life was new for his time. Or rather, that he was renewing for himself and his brothers the old way of life of the earliest disciples of Christ.[15] Although Francis was able to maintain his vision this time, he was certain to have to fight for it in the future. It was at this Chapter that the brothers agreed to go beyond countries that were already Christian and set out for non-Christian lands. They went to Tunis and Morocco and Francis himself chose Egypt.[16]

Part Two: Francis and the Saracens

Throughout the years that Francis was attracting an expanding brotherhood, Pope Innocent III was planning a 5th crusade. By 1213 his plan was made public for a crusade to take place from 1217 to 1221. It was impossible for Francis and his friars to avoid hearing the sermons that were being preached in all the churches and the prayers for the liberation of Jerusalem from the Saracens. All Christians were being called to participate.

The Pope preached the crusades as a way of imitating Christ and as a holy war against the Saracens who he perceived as Christ's enemies. The Holy Land belonged to Christ and the Pope promised salvation to those who offered their lives in Christ's name.[17]

Francis also wanted to be a martyr, to lose his life for his Lord, to be a knight battling for the sake of the Kingdom. But despite the strength and influence of the Pope's call to arms, Francis had a very different vision of God. He chose as his weapons a message of peace and the hope for conversion. In fact, Francis had twice before attempted to travel to the East to approach the "enemy" with his message of peace. His was a very different kind of crusade. In 1211 he set out for Syria but was shipwrecked on the Dalmatian coast in a storm. Francis was forced to return to Italy as a stowaway on another ship because he had no money for his passage. Once again in 1213 he wanted to go to Morocco to preach to the Saracens, but this time he got sick and was forced to return home.

Pope Innocent lll died on July 18, 1216 and the newly elected Pope, Honorius lll, continued preparations for the crusade. As history has proved over and over again, making war against another nation requires a united stance. The Pope recognized that the civil wars and rivalries over property among the Christians of Western Europe were a deterrent to his goal. He reinforced Pope Innocent's decree that peace be declared for 4 years throughout the Christian world by threatening excommunication and the seizing of property. In 1217 he appointed Cardinal Hugolino to oversee his efforts to unite the many Italian factions and communes in support for the crusades.

By this time Francis had begun to send his brothers out to other Christian countries and he himself chose to travel to France. Trusting that God would provide for them, the brothers travelled without possessions and were instructed to enter every house with their greeting of peace. When Cardinal Hugolino met Francis in Florence he ordered him to return to Rome suggesting that there were clerics in Rome who objected to the rapidly expanding brotherhood. Apparently Francis replied that he would be ashamed to send his brothers to other countries without going himself. The Cardinal retorted that he had no right to send his brothers off to die of hunger. Francis' reply shows us just how differently he understood his desire to imitate Christ from that preached by the Pope in recruiting for his crusade. Francis said that the friars were called to preach salvation to all the world and that they would be received by believers and unbelievers alike. If they held to their promise to embrace poverty and trust entirely in their Lord, God would certainly give them all that they needed.[18]

In fact, those who defended the crusades preached with righteousness that to kill the Saracens in the name of Christ and regain the holy city of Jerusalem was a means to salvation, and a war sanctioned by God. This was the policy of the church and all Christians were expected to participate. Although some Saracens did convert to Christianity out of fear of the powerful Christian army, conversion was not the Pope's primary goal. Demonizing the enemy is always a strategy in war. That Francis went to Egypt with neither weapons nor possessions and did not speak or write a negative word about Mohammad or Islam at any time is an amazing testimony to his courage to ignore the powerful forces around him and obey his inner experience of faith in a God who loves all people. In taking the Gospel message literally, Francis came as a peacemaker, understanding nonviolence as Jesus' way to salvation.[19]

On June 24, 1219 Francis left Italy for the city of Damietta situated near the mouth of the Nile in Egypt. From 853 this city had served as a port of connection, containing a naval fleet of ships charged with preventing the continual attempts of Christians to land. They came from Byzantium at first and then the crusaders came from the Roman Empire.[20] The crusaders captured the city in November of 1219. When Francis arrived at Damietta the Sultan, Malik al-Kamil was encamped south of Damietta at a place called al-Marssura.[21] Apparently Francis stayed in Damietta for several months preaching to the army and many were moved to join the brothers. Then

Francis asked for permission to go to the Saracen camp.

Francis received permission to go to the Saracen camp but he was told that he was going at his own risk. There may even have been an understanding that anyone who attempted to convert the Muslims to Christianity would be executed. Whether this was true or not, attempting to cross over to the Saracen camp during a war was risking being killed. Francis took one of his brothers with him and apparently they were captured by soldiers who mistook them for a military emissary. They were taken to the Sultan as Francis had hoped. His intent was to convert the Sultan and although he didn't succeed, he was apparently heard. In fact, the Sultan gave him permission to travel to the Holy Land unharmed and then had him and his brother politely escorted back to the Christian camp. On August 27, 1221 the crusaders were forced to surrender and the fifth crusade ended in failure.

Francis did visit the Holy Land before returning via the seaport, Acre. In Acre he learned that the first Franciscan friars were martyred preaching the Gospel in Marrakesch, Morocco on January 16, 1220. He also learned that while he was away the Order was facing a crisis in Italy. He returned to Venice where he asked the help of Cardinal Hugolino who was appointed Protector of the Order by the Pope. From then on Francis struggled to uphold the vision expressed in his first Rule in 1209 against the differing views of newer and more educated members. Communities were now being established in many countries and the Order included thousands of brothers. Due to his long journey, his past illnesses, and quite likely to his long hours of prayer and days of fasting, Francis was beginning to lose his health.

So many people were drawn to Francis and his vision of the Gospel that he wrote a letter, which he called a "Letter to the Faithful" in which he began to outline a way of life for people who desired to follow his vision, but needed to remain in the secular world. Not feeling well enough to visit them personally, he wrote this letter to the first brothers and sisters who came to him asking for penance and wishing to follow his way of life. It led to the establishment of a Third Order of Franciscans.[22] As always, Francis quotes the Gospel extensively in his sermons and in his writing, and in this letter he repeats his favorite themes.

In 1221, with the help of Cardinal Hugolino, Francis wrote a Rule for the secular Third Order. It includes recommendations to dress simply and discreetly, avoid too worldly amusements, to pray daily and fast often. They were advised to receive Communion, confess their sins, and to gather once a month to attend Mass and pray together. They were to give money to the poor and the sick, pay their own debts and be reconciled with their enemies. They agreed not to bear arms or make any solemn oaths without the permission of the Pope. The Rule also included recommendations for organizing the Third Order community with elections of ministers and other designated roles. A special bond was formed between Francis and this community as they identified themselves as followers of the Poverello. The Third Order communities and individuals following their Rule began to be established wherever there were Franciscans and Poor Clares.[23]

Meanwhile Francis continued to try to create a Rule for the Brotherhood that would finally be agreed to by the dissenting members of the community, maintain his Gospel vision, and be approved of by Rome. He went to one of his hermitages along with Brother Leo, who wrote for him, and immersed himself in prayer and fasting, struggling to write from his heart without his usual references to the Gospel. The documents he produced were questioned and disputed in the Order until Cardinal Hugolino finally put them into their final form. At last, on November 29, 1223 Pope Honorius gave his approval and the Friars Minor had their final Rule. Yet his biographers note that Francis had to compromise his original idealistic vision to achieve the goal. From then on the Friars were no longer as poor and entirely dependent on God as Francis and his brothers had been in the early days at Rivo Torto.[24] Francis spent the rest of his life taking every opportunity to show his friars by his own example what their call to poverty and humility required of them. In his own way he continued to resist the changes that increasingly allowed the brothers to live more comfortably.

In August of 1224 Francis and some of his closest companions went on retreat to the hermitage at Mount La Verna high in the Apennine mountains. Francis was not strong enough for the rigorous journey and exhaustion forced him to borrow a donkey. Sensing that he was nearing the end of his life, Francis came to this solitary place in order to pray alone to his God, before whom he continued to feel the pain of his own sins. In a solitary hut some distance from the hermitage he began to fast and pray. It is clear that Francis' greatest desire was to imitate the life of Christ in his own. His biographers say that it was at La Verna that he began to experience visions of his Lord's Passion and death on the cross. They say that on September 14th he prayed to experience Christ's pain and saw a vision of an angel called a Seraph nailed to the cross. He was deeply affected by this vision. While he searched his own heart for the meaning of it he received the same wounds in his own body that he saw in the vision. He carefully hid these marks from his companions.[25]

At the end of September Francis returned to the Porziuncola, and then, despite his weakness and increasing illnesses he preached in the towns and villages of Umbria through the winter. By the spring he was almost blind and was taken to San Damiano to be cared for by Sister Clare. This was the last time that he would see her. After some weeks he agreed to go to Rietti for medical treatment, and later to Sienna, but the treatments ultimately increased his suffering. In the spring of 1226, fearing that he was close to death he dictated his last testament at the hermitage at Cortona. He wanted to die at the Porziuncola and on the way there he passed through Assisi and gave his blessing to his home town. Throughout these last days and weeks Francis continued to share his passionate vision for his friars with them and composed some of his most memorable poetry and songs. He sang this song to the virtue of humility:

> "O sublime humility! O humble sublimity!
> The Lord of the universe, God and the Son of God,
> so humbles Himself that for our salvation
> He hides Himself under an ordinary piece of bread!
> Brothers, look at the humility of God,
> and pour out your hearts before Him!
> Humble yourselves that you may be exalted by Him!
> Hold back nothing of yourselves for yourselves,
> that He Who gives Himself totally to you
> may receive you totally!" [26]

Francis was so caught up in his love affair with God that he saw his lover in all of creation. He felt his kinship with the sun as a brother and with the moon as a sister. He preached to the birds and befriended wild animals as he sensed that all living things are gifts of God. He treasured every scrap of paper because the words written on them contained the letters of God's name. Francis found a way to express the joy he felt even in the midst of physical and emotional suffering. Out of the depth of his sorrow for what he perceived as his own sinfulness came his resounding joy at God's mercy and forgiveness. Finally, he even welcomed death itself, which he considered a "second death," the first being his total submission to his God. He personifies death as a sister, praising his God for her coming near the end of his life in "The Canticle of the Creatures" written in 1225.

> "Praised be You, my Lord, through our
>   Sister Bodily Death,
> from whom no one living can escape.
> Woe to those who die in mortal sin.
> Blessed are those whom death will find
>   in Your most holy will,
> for the second death shall do them no harm."

At the Porziuncola on October 3, 1226 Francis asked the

brothers to read the Passion from the Gospel according to John. It is likely that he wanted to hear the story of the Last Supper and to pray Psalm 141. As the sun went down, the Poverello died. He was 44 years old.

On July 19, 1228 Francis was declared a saint by his friend and supporter, Cardinal Hugolino, who had become Pope Gregory IX in 1227. Francis was declared the patron saint of Italy in 1939. In 1980, Pope John Paul II brought the Poverello into our contemporary world by making him patron saint of ecology.

Part Three: The Spirit of a Saint

When Louis Massignon renewed his friendship with Mary Kahil in Egypt in 1934, he took one more step towards living out his religious convictions. She too was a Christian who spent her life in the Islamic world and centered her interests on connecting with Muslims, especially the women. The bond between these two Christians who devoted their lives to the Muslims resulted in the exchange of more than a thousand letters by the time of Massignon's death in 1962. These passionate exchanges resulted in his most inspired writings about the depth of his faith experience. The letters were filled with intense spiritual reflections and discussions about the establishment of their educational and spiritual organization in Cairo dedicated to Muslim Christian relations called the Badaliya. This prayer group grew out of their shared faith experience and began on a trip to Damietta on February 9, 1934. Kneeling together before the altar in a small church they renewed their vow made 21 years before to offer their lives to God in substitution for the Muslim people.[27]

For Louis Massignon, the city of Damietta on the coast of the Mediterranean Sea was a place where many of his own spiritual connections seemed to converge. It was the birthplace of Mary Kahil. By renewing their friendship and spiritual bond here in Damietta they gave birth to the Badaliya. Both wrote how the fire of their individual vocations was passionately rekindled in meeting each other once again. Saint Louis, after whom Louis Massignon was named, was once imprisoned here in 1250. For many years Massignon had searched for the tomb of the Islamic mystical love poet, Shushtari and found it here in Damietta. And of course it was Saint Francis' visit to the Islamic sultan in Damietta that inspired Massignon's vocation as a Third Order Franciscan. It was fitting for Louis Massignon and Mary Kahil to come here to give birth again to their bond of friendship; a connectedness to one another that can only be understood as a deep and committed sharing of mystical love.[28] It was the kind of mystical love that Francis tried to teach his brothers and express in his songs and poetry.

Poverty

One compelling reason for Massignon to embrace the Poverello was the fact that Francis was one of the world's great lovers of God. Just as he was drawn to Hallaj by the intensity of the Muslim mystic's passion for God that ended in a violent death making him a martyr, so he would be attracted to Francis, the troubadour whose love affair with God spilled over into loving all of creation. He even suffered the wounds of Christ in his longing to heal the world. Francis chose poverty as a way of life because he, like Charles de Foucauld, saw in the image of Jesus and His mother God's choosing to come into the world in poverty, subject as we all are to the care and concern of others. Francis wrote about Jesus in his letter to the Faithful:

> "Though He was rich, He wished, together with the most Blessed Virgin, His mother, to choose poverty in the world, beyond all else."[29]

We know that physical poverty leads to terrible deprivations in our world. Even in the wealthiest nations of the world the children of homeless families suffer from diseases related to malnutrition and learning disabilities from poor attendance in school. Poverty is not a state of being that most of us tolerate, much less desire. When we are physically poor it reminds us of how dependent we are on God and one another. Spiritual poverty challenges our illusions of power and control confronting us with the reality that human beings are fragile and easily damaged physically and emotionally. Francis seemed to understand that Jesus had to come into the world as poor and dependent in order to truly experience what we experience and to help us to recognize just how poor we are without God. If Francis was to imitate the life of Jesus, then he too would have to be poor in order to show us how to thrive on God's abundant love.

> "Lady holy Poverty, may the Lord protect you
> Holy Poverty confounds the desire for riches, greed,
> and the cares of this world."[30]

Francis called her Lady Poverty and spoke of her as a virtue that would give his brothers a way to approach others in peace.

Peace

> "When the brothers go through the world, let them take nothing for the journey, neither knapsack, nor purse, nor bread, nor money, nor walking stick. Whatever house they enter, let them first say: Peace to this house."[31]

For Francis to take the gospel message literally meant that he was to bring its message of peace into a world that in many ways resembles our own. Francis chose gospel texts that expressed his experience of how he felt called to live in a world that valued property and possessions over relationships with others, and promoted violence in dealing with one's perceived enemies. He recognized that the way to enter into the minds and hearts of others was to share life with them rather than compete for possessions or preach to them. By owning nothing and bringing no possessions with him he removed one of the major reasons for division and conflict between people. If there were no property or possessions to fight over perhaps people would find another way to relate to each other. His greeting of peace as he entered a house was an invitation and a way of creating peace in the world, one household at a time. There was no way that Francis could follow Jesus by taking up arms against the Saracens. He visited the sultan with the same message of peace that he offered when he entered the homes of villagers in Italy. By living this way of peace Francis and his brothers radically challenged the social system around them and the church as well.

> "Let them not resist anyone evil, but whoever strikes them on one cheek, let them offer him the other as well. Whoever takes their cloak, let them not withhold their tunic. Let them give to all who ask of them and whoever takes what is theirs, let them not seek to take it back."[32]

Francis' way of peace was radical. He believed that peace would never be accomplished with violence. When the brothers were attacked or persecuted he told them to remember their Lord who was crucified for them. It was a great lesson in humility that allowed the brothers to maintain their highest value of peaceful sharing of life. Francis felt the peace of God so deeply within him that he wanted all others to receive that peace when they met him. Eight hundred years before Gandhi created a revolution in India by living his belief in nonviolence in an effort, in part, to heal the divisions between Hindus and Muslims, Francis and his brothers refused to take up arms against the Saracens. He said that his mission of peace was meant for all people, believers and unbelievers alike.

Louis Massignon spent many years studying Arabic and Islam and searching in Muslim countries for sources for *The Passion of al-Hallaj*. His friendships and close understanding and identification with Islamic culture ultimately also became a nonviolent mission of peace. When he marched in the streets of Paris in his seventies for the cause of Algerian independence from the French colonial views of his time he too was refusing to take up arms against the Saracens.

> "The Lord says; Behold I am sending you like sheep in the midst of wolves. Therefore be prudent as serpents and simple as doves. Let any brother, then, who desires by divine inspiration to go among the Saracens and other nonbelievers, go..."[33]

Francis heard all around him that the Saracens were like wolves, an enemy to be feared. But his own experience was to risk going among them as a sheep, unarmed with anything but the strength of the peace he came to offer them. When Francis visited the sultan he was not treated as an enemy but rather treated with respect, offered the gift of safe journey back to the crusader's camp, and even to the Holy Land. In fact, Francis had warned the crusaders accurately that they would be defeated in a battle on August 29, 1219, after which sultan al-Malek al-Kamil made a peace offering to the crusaders which was unfortunately rejected by cardinal Pelagius.[34] Francis discovered that the "wolves" were willing to treat the "sheep" with respect and even negotiate peace.

One of the most meaningful experiences at the very beginning of Louis Massignon's spiritual conversion was his realization of the kind of hospitality offered to him by his Muslim friends, the Allussys. Not only did they provide safe passage and physical protection at great personal risk, but they also prayed for him. Hallaj was not his only Muslim intercessor.

> "As for the brothers who go, they can live spiritually among the Saracens and other nonbelievers in two ways. One way is not to engage in arguments or disputes but to be subject to every human creature for God's sake... The other way is to announce the word of God when they see that it pleases the Lord..."[35]

Francis suggests that everything we do should be for the sake of God, even putting aside our instincts to defend our own faith beliefs which leads to arguments and even war. Instead he asks us to be Friars Minor, lesser brothers, subjecting, submitting, putting ourselves aside, that others may have the space to be themselves in our presence. Being subject to one another, rather than giving one person power over another, allows us to live with one another. In fact, Francis went beyond his insistence that the brothers be respectful of one another in this way, to expecting them to treat every person and all of creation in this spirit. Living our faith in God's loving presence in our lives is a far more powerful weapon than arguments or disputes. It may even lead to others wanting to know what inspires us to live the way we do. Only then can we be sure that it is the right time to speak of our Christian faith and beliefs.

This was one of the most conflictual challenges for Massignon in his life. There was a tension between his belief in Christ as the ultimate way to God and his respect for Muslims and their faith in Islam. He was, after all, still influenced by the religious norms of his time. It was through the Badaliya, and his consistent dedication to praying for the Muslim people that he struggled with his ambivalence.

Chapter Five

The Feminine Spirit
Mary Kahil and the Substitutes

LOUIS MASSIGNON'S RELATIONSHIP with Egypt began early in his life. When he was 13 years old he met Henri Maspero in school. Henri was the son of the well-known Egyptologist, Gaston Maspero. The two boys were both eager to learn about cultures outside of Western Europe and it was in Gaston Maspero's library that Louis first began to develop his interest in the languages and culture of the Middle East. Henri Maspero became a lifelong friend. When Louis went to Cairo for the first time in 1906 to spend a year in an Arabic speaking country, he became a member of the French Institute of Oriental Archeology. Gaston Maspero was the director and Henri was there studying Egyptology. Henri's father supported Louis' original plan to study Egyptian archeology.

During this year in Egypt Louis discovered the Islamic mystic, al-Hallaj and changed the direction of his research to the study of the 10th century Islamic Saint. Cairo ultimately became the ground where both his intellectual and spiritual life began to take root. Louis' intense conversion experience in Baghdad in 1908 resulted in his private vow to remain chaste and devote his life to God. When he returned to Cairo in 1913 to teach he was in the midst of his struggle to balance his desire for a religious vocation with his growing reputation as a scholar. He met the young Egyptian woman, Mary Kahil, and invited her to join him in prayer, offering themselves in mystical substitution for the conversion of their Spanish friend Luis de Cuadra. From the beginning Massignon was drawn to those medieval saints and mystics in each generation that Huysmans described as being chosen to offer themselves in mystical substitution for the salvation of the world.

In January, 1934 when Louis Massignon returned to Cairo to become one of the five members of the European Academy of Arabic, he renewed his friendship with Mary Kahil. In a letter written on January 10th he wrote that after 21 years he felt the burning intensity of his conversion experience return and once again felt tormented by his desire to be holy and belong to God alone.[1] This return to Egypt where his spiritual life first began to take shape has an ironic sense of destiny when seen in the context of this ancient part of the world which gave birth to the three monotheistic traditions. All three, Judaism, Christianity and Islam would also give birth to Massignon's academic studies and deeply influence his own spiritual life.

Mary Kahil inevitably brought her cultural and religious heritage into her relationship with Louis Massignon and each appeared to inspire the other with their shared experiences of Christianity and Islam. In establishing the Badaliya on February 9th, in Damietta, Massignon rediscovered his vocation of mystical substitution. As he had in 1913, he invited Mary Kahil to share his calling with him. Just as Massignon discovered the heart of his spirituality in Egypt so Mary Kahil's life story finds its meaning in this ancient land as well.

Egypt:[2]

In the Northeast corner of Africa where the Nile river cuts the desert plateau into the eastern and western desert, Egypt claims the fertile Nile valley and delta for 95% of her population. Ancient Egypt flourished for 3000 years under the rule of 31 consecutive dynasties reaching the height of her powers in 2000 BC. The dynasties began to rise and fall with the invasions of foreign powers and still her civilization and artistic expression thrived, and worship of the gods survived, until the rise of the Roman Empire.

For one brief 17 year period from 1353 to 1336 BC a Pharaoh named Akhenaten had a new vision of art and religious worship. From the ancient tradition of many gods with different powers represented in both animal and human form Akhenaten chose to worship one aspect of the sun god, Aten, "the light within the sun's disc." He saw Aten as the sole creator of the universe. He built a new city designed to worship the light as the sun rose through the cliffs on the horizon. He lived there with his beautiful wife Nefertiti and their children. When he died the city was destroyed and when his son, prince Tutankhaten became Pharaoh he returned to the ancient Egyptian traditions. Akhenaten was considered a heretic and was all but forgotten except perhaps for the religion of a tribal people in the desert who came to worship one God, settled in Egypt and were then condemned by the Pharaoh to slavery. In about 1250 BC there was a great Exodus as the Hebrew people followed Moses out of Egypt.

When Alexander the Great invaded Egypt in 332 BC he founded the city of Alexandria. It became a center for the diversity and plurality of the Hellenistic age which continued for 300 years after his death. The city soon became known for Greek scholarship and science as well as Semitic learning and remained a cultural center throughout the dynasty of the Ptolemies who succeeded Alexander. Thirty years before the birth of Christ the last Egyptian empire under the Ptolemy dynasty fell to the Roman Empire.

If Egypt once welcomed the Hebrew people, and then enslaved them, it also became a land of asylum some 30 years after the Romans conquered Egypt when a poor family from a small town called Nazareth in Palestine sought refuge there from the tyranny of a King called Herod. The story of Mary and Joseph's flight into Egypt to protect their child Jesus from harm is perhaps a foreshadowing of the welcome that Christians would later receive there. From the 1st century in our era Christianity was present in Egypt. Many of the most famous early theologians and philosophers, known as the Desert Fathers in the Church, were Egyptians.

The Romans held Egypt until 395 AD placing Byzantine Constantinople in control of the country. In 313 Constantine gave Christians permission to worship without persecution and a formal Egyptian church was established. Before the Arab conquest in the 7th century the Egyptians spoke Greek and were known in the West as Copts. The Byzantine Empire fell when the Arabs invaded in 642 and Egypt became an Arabic speaking state with Islam as its dominant religion. When the Egyptian Muslims no longer identified themselves as Copt it became the term applied to the Christian minority.

Egypt continued to fall under foreign rule, to the Ottoman Turks in 1517 and to France in 1798. The British joined the Turks forcing Napoleon to withdraw and the struggle for political and economic influence in Egypt intensified. In 1805 Mohammad Ali became governor but also put the country in debt to the British who took control in 1882 and made Egypt a British protectorate in 1914. Egypt's independence in 1922 brought the establishment of a monarchy that was overthrown in 1952 by Nassar. He was the first native Egyptian to rule in 2000 years.

Mary Kahil's Egypt in the early 20th century was a country of dramatic contrasts as it is today. The old city of Cairo, with its ancient mosques overshadowing the dusty roadways, is lined with whole families living in poverty in crudely fashioned huts. This shocks our Western sensibilities. Along the Nile river luxury hotels gleam in the sun serving the wealthy multicultural population. The busy port of Alexandria is teeming with people crowding through the open marketplace where everything, from produce to gold, is being loudly displayed. Egypt's cities have seen multiple political revolutions, international tensions and wars, and still its glorious ancient history rises up in the desert, visible in the great pyramids and the mysterious gigantic sphinx.

Most of the Christians in Muslim Egypt belong to the Coptic Orthodox Church. There is a small community, however, originally made up of Greek colonists and Christians from Syria and Egypt who adopted Arabic culture and are known as Melkite Christians. They practiced the Byzantine religious rites and in 1054 followed the patriarch of Constantinople into schism with Rome. Those who reunified with Rome in 1724 are known as Greek Catholic Melkites. They practice the Byzantine liturgical celebration in Arabic.

Part One: Mary Kahil

Mary Kahil was born in Damietta, Egypt on January 28, 1889. Her ancestors came from Syria in 1775 to settle in Damietta and Alexandria. They were educated in European universities and held important government offices when Mohammad Ali became governor of Egypt in 1805. Mary's father, Constantin Kahil, was a successful businessman in wholesale lumber. He married a German woman in Damietta and they had five children.

In an interview at the age of 82 Mary described some of her childhood memories.[3] The family spent the summers in a large old house with 12 or 13 rooms in Damietta. Every evening Mary would sit on cushions playing with her dolls on the wide balcony listening to the chant of the Muezzin calling the Muslims to prayer. They sang praises to God and Mary found herself carried away by the sound and its harmony and felt at peace. Close to the house there was a very high Minaret belonging to a 14th century Andalusian Mosque. Mary was struck by the wooden triangles on the side of the Minaret where the birds rested. She thought that it was very moving that Islam made a place for the birds to pray on the side of their Mosque. Her nurse, Mabrouka, was Muslim. Mary and her family were Greek Catholic Melkite Christians.

Mary felt there was a sense of community and sympathy among the Muslims and Christians in Damietta. She remembers her mother visiting the Muslim women in their venetian style homes. Her mother spoke Arabic very well but her husband would not allow her to learn to write. When they returned to Cairo Mary went to a school run by religious sisters called the Mother of God. Later she was sent to Beirut to attend a school run by the Sisters of Nazareth. She was surprised to find that Arabic was taught every afternoon for three hours. Mary was falling asleep because she did not yet know how to read Arabic. She and her friend Linda Yared became "revolutionaries" protesting against the western culture imposed in the schools by the French.

In 1905, when she was 17 years old Mary's father died and she returned to Cairo. She found the house full of relatives and her mother lying in her bed and very unhappy. Mary was sent back to Lebanon to finish school. In 1909 when she was 20 she returned to Cairo. She describes herself as very mentally active with a great desire to do something useful. She wrote a feminist pamphlet in which she stated, "We Arab women only wish to speak Arabic. We wish to put our traditions, customs and language back in a place of honor." A friend who was a lawyer told her about another woman who would be able to help her. Mary describes Houda Chaaraoui as an elegant 40-year-old woman who lived in a European style house. Mary told Houda that she wanted to hold conferences for Egyptian women to discuss their origins and talk about Arab history. Houda was surprised that Mary was a Christian and an Arab. They found a French woman named Mme. Chevalier who arranged conferences. They held their conferences at the home of the princess Bazla Ali which Mary describes as a marvellous palace.

Mary was invited to become the secretary for the Mohammad Ali Association because she could write in French. From then on she found herself in the midst of Muslim society. She met many Muslim women and was astonished to find herself so popular with them. Mary had a car and was free to go where she liked whereas the Muslim women were not allowed to go out. At the same time that she was involved with the Muslim women Mary also worked for Christian charities with the Sisters of Saint Vincent de Paul. There she met a charming Spanish woman, the Countess de Hohenwaert. Her husband was with the Austrian Consulate. Because Mary had an Austrian passport the two women found a connection. Mary became close friends with Countess de Hohenwaert's niece, Mélita Talbot, and Carmen, the daughter of the Ambassador of Spain. They were often invited for dinner at the home of the Countess. It was at the home of Countess de Hohenwaert that Mary first met Louis Massignon. She was 25 years old and he was 29.

On the evening of December 11, 1912 the Countess told Mary that she was seating her next to an "Arab" with whom she would be able to speak Arabic. When Louis told her that he had just come from the opening of a French school in Syria called the Joan of Arc and that he had worked towards bringing French culture to Syria, she was irate. "We are born enemies," she said. Their first meeting was an argument at the table, but they continued to meet often at evenings with the Hohenwaerts. One time Louis asked her if she prayed often and went to Mass everyday. "Why?" she asked.

A Spanish friend of Louis Massignon, Luis de Cuadra, also came to the Hohenwaerts often. He had left his Christian upbringing to become a Muslim. Mary describes his mother, the Marquise de Guadalmina, as a ravishing, white haired woman of 55. She and the Marquise often went to the movies together. When Luis became sick with Typhus and had to be hospitalized, his mother asked everyone to pray for his recovery. When it appeared that Luis was going to die, Massignon said to Mary, "You are sad because Luis is going to die; but make a sacrifice for him! Make the sacrifice of your life." Mary didn't understand. Louis explained that he was inviting her to offer her life in mystical substitution so that Luis would be converted back to Christianity. Although Mary agreed to make this vow with Massignon she admitted that she was more interested in Luis' recovering his health. However she and Massignon had learned to pray together and the seed was planted for the beginning of the Badaliya.

Caught in the midst of the intensity of his own recent conversion experience Louis struggled with his sense of sinfulness and desire to remain chaste for God. He was afraid that Mary was going to become too attached to him and decided to return to France so as not to see her. The Countess de Hohenwaert tried to dissuade him from leaving. Massignon wrote in his journal, "I left the debate, troubled, outraged to have felt this unexpected feminine attack weaken my sinful misogyny, which since my conversion had found common cause with my perceived need for an ascetic 'manichean' stance. Content to retreat soon enough in order not to make anyone suffer, I recited the Magnificat."[4] Later he wrote to the Countess that he had decided to marry his cousin. He married Marcelle Dansaert-Testelin on January 27, 1914. Mary did not see Louis Massignon again until 1934.

In 1913, Mary and her mother and brothers and sisters left for Europe where they remained throughout World War 1. At the end of the War she went to London and in 1920 she returned to Cairo. When Mary got off the boat she kissed the ground of her beloved Egypt and the shipyard workers applauded. At home her friend Houda Chaaraoui came to see her. Houda told Mary that they had established a Feminist Union and invited her to join them. Mary reminded Houda that it was she who approached her friend years before with her feminist pamphlet, thus Mary was included as a founder of the Feminist Union.

Aligned with the suffragettes in London the Egyptian women worked towards social and political reform for women's rights. They protested in the streets of Cairo and went to Rome for an International Women's Congress in 1923. Their goals included assuring education for girls, voting rights, reforms of religious laws, including limiting or abolishing polygamy and eliminating the required veil. They worked towards changing divorce regulations and gaining public office and assuring equal rights for Egyptian women. At the same time they struggled against British colonialism.

Mary knew that she could do many things with her abundant energy, spontaneity, and ability to think quickly and efficiently. Along with the Feminist Union she once again went to work for the Mohammad Ali Association. One day she received a card with a brief message from Louis Massignon, "With respectful memories." Shortly afterwards while at tea she learned that Louis was in Cairo and went to find him at the Archeological Institute. It was January 29, 1934. Mary described how she felt when she went with him to Mass the next day. At the moment of Communion Massignon said, "Come, receive Communion." She found herself in what she called "an unknown state, a very different sense of well being, completely strange for me."

When Massignon asked her what she was doing with her life, she told him that she didn't keep herself occupied with Christian projects but rather with Muslim organizations like Mohammad Ali and the Feminist Union. This was the way that she tried to connect with Egyptian Muslim women. She was surprised when he told her that this was her vocation. "But I don't have a religious vocation!" she said. He replied that her vocation was to be involved with the Muslims. It seemed to Mary that Massignon had affirmed her in her path when he told her that she had a vocation to live among the Muslims. From then on she devoted herself to them. She told him the names of all her friends and every night he prayed for them, especially for a young Muslim woman who had died in childbirth.

Mary described how she felt attached to Massignon as a spiritual guide rather than as a man. She said, "It was like an unsolicited silent call in the depth of myself." One day she asked him why he had not become a priest. He told her that his confessor had asked him to get married and he had obeyed. She was astonished that a man Massignon's age still obeyed his confessor. But he also shared with her that he had always wanted to be a priest in order to be closer to the Lord Jesus. When Mary told him that it was still possible he replied, "I will think about it."

The Vow[5]

On February 9th they went to a Franciscan church in Damietta. Mary described the three large windows in this church that look out on the Nile with the palm trees swaying behind them. She said, "I prayed there with intense devotion, enchanted in a way that is difficult to explain." She expressed her feelings towards the Arabs who had made Islam the dominant religion in Egypt. "I told Massignon how sad I was to see this city where so many Syrian Christians had come, where my ancestors had lived, and where none of them are left. I was leaning against the altar columns and Massignon said, 'You are marked for a vow. So make one.' But what vow? 'One that loves them.' I said to him, 'That's impossible'. He then told me that there is nothing closer to hate than love. 'Make a vow, one that gives your life for them.' In a state of exaltation that is impossible to relive, I made the vow to live for them, to give my life for them, to stand in their place before the throne of Jesus, and that all my life and all my eternity I would ask for them to be enlightened. Massignon took my hand. He made the same vow. We made this vow with a fervor, an illumination that I no longer know. When we left the church I was transformed. I was no longer myself. I was like a life ablaze. While walking I found an immense carpenter's nail. I picked it up and gave it to Massignon. 'Why this nail?' I said to him, 'To pierce your heart'. He took the nail and put it in his pocket."

They returned to Cairo exhausted and went directly to the Jesuit Fathers' house. There they found Father de Bonneville. Mary said to him, "Massignon and I have made a vow. We have offered ourselves for the Muslims. Not to convert them but so that the will of God be done in them and through them. We want to make our prayer theirs, our lives theirs, and present them to the Lord." He said, "Please, take me with you, I will be the third." I can't express our joy, our comfort, in hearing these words of Father de Bonneville, who I loved so much and who was my confessor. We clung to his arm, we were happy, all of life had changed for me." Until then nothing seemed to predict such a mysterious vocation for a wealthy woman like Mary who was so prominent in Egyptian society. And it was only slowly that she grew from her friendship with Muslim women to joining Massignon in his vocation of love for them that he called "mystical substitution."⁶

Part Two: The Badaliya

On July 18, 1934 Massignon received an acknowledgment from Pope Pius Xl of their vow at Damietta and he felt that his vocation had been blessed. For him the Badaliya (from the Arabic word meaning a substitute, or to put oneself in the place of another), was a way of living out the vocation that he had felt himself called to from the time of his conversion. Now he understood it as an offering to live his life for Islam and the Arab world. It began with a vow that he and Mary repeated each year in Damietta on Massignon's annual trip to Cairo. Others joined the small prayer group of Christians living in the midst of the Islamic Middle East, and Mary and Massignon understood them as having a particular responsibility in relation to their Muslim brothers and sisters. As a minority, Arab Christians suffered persecution and discrimination. The goal of the Badaliya was to take to heart Christ's words to love one's enemies and to pray for those who persecute you.⁷ As Christians they believed that they were reconciled to God through the death of God's son, even if they had rejected Him.⁸ They wanted to give themselves to Jesus in the name of their Muslim brothers and sisters, hoping that divine grace would assure their salvation as well.⁹ Many men and women living in monastic communities in France and other parts of the world also joined them by offering themselves in the spirit of the Badaliya.

Mary and Massignon had rediscovered a value that is basic to Christianity and a path towards God. In her personal journal Mary wrote, "How shall I speak of the beginning of this Badaliya in which the roots and the seeds were buried in the first years of my childhood for such a long time? I must even go back to the source of my life."¹⁰ For Massignon the inspiration for the Badaliya first began with the prayers of his mother and Huysmans, and the intercession of Hallaj, for his own conversion in 1908. He had no doubt that Charles de Foucauld was asking him to complete for him what was lacking in

Foucauld's passion and death in 1916, by inspiring him to suffer for the Muslims and Arabs. He felt that his vows as a Third Order Franciscan in 1931 and the influence of Saint Francis gave shape to the Badaliya by providing a sense of self-sacrifice at its root.[11]

Massignon was only in Cairo once a year. His letters to Mary guided and inspired her deepening relationship with God. Writing to her seemed to encourage his ability to express the longing and painful internal struggle of desiring to give himself entirely to the Love that is God, while simultaneously fulfilling his demanding family and career obligations. Theirs was a shared mystical journey. Both continued to live their daily lives, he primarily in Paris and she in Cairo.

Mary devoted herself to improving life for Egyptian women and took on many projects including establishing medical clinics in poor neighborhoods. She organized and headed up volunteers to care for victims of malaria and cholera epidemics and convinced a private hospital to provide training for nursing students. She supported the education of a Christian Egyptian youth organization by providing social, religious, and cultural journals to inspire them to become socially active in the community. She and Father Ayrout re-established the Association of Schools in Upper Egypt to provide primary and adult education, health services and economic development for coptic Christians.

In 1939 Massignon included a pilgrimage to the tomb of Hallaj in Baghdad on his annual trip to Cairo. The threat of war in Europe only allowed him one last visit before being called into the army once again at the age of 57. For the next five years he would be cut off from the Arab world which he called his "homeland" and the annual renewal and nourishment of his vocation of Badaliya.[12]

In 1941, in the midst of the devastation of World War II, Mary bought an abandoned Anglican church in the center of Cairo and transformed it into a Byzantine rite church which she named Our Lady of Peace. She also wanted Egyptian Christians to be visible in this predominantly Muslim society.

In 1942 she paid for the restoration of the oldest Greek Melkite church in Damietta which had been abandoned in 1910. She organized an annual pilgrimage attracting hundreds of Christians from all social classes. In 1944, after the second world war, Mary and her sister went with Christian, Jewish and Muslim friends from this multireligious community on a pilgrimage to Jerusalem. She continued to meet with the Badaliya for their weekly hour of prayer and was finally able to resume writing to Massignon. His first letter to her was filled with the pain of the loss of friends who were deported, imprisoned or killed, the illnesses caused by so much deprivation, and the suffering he experienced at being separated from the Arab and Muslim countries where he had wished one day to die. At that moment he could not see an end to the suffering nor his isolation.[13] He was moving more and more towards the nonviolent philosophy and solution to conflict chosen by Gandhi. When he was once again able to travel to the Middle East, a changing world compelled him into the political activity of his last years. By 1945 he was once again corresponding with friends and returned to his pre-war intellectual life of prolific lecturing and writing. He was sent on a six month trip by the French government to renew relations with the Middle Eastern countries.[14]

Massignon was finally able to return to Cairo and the Badaliya. Mary had put the rectory of Our Lady of Peace in a house next to the church and she and Massignon established a center there called Dar as-Salam, The House of Peace. Mary wanted The House of Peace to be dedicated with equal fidelity to both the Christian and Arab worlds. It sponsored over 130 international conferences discussing Egyptology, Hellenism, philosophy, ecumenism, theology, the lives of the saints, and mysticism, along with fulfilling Mary's desire to encourage awareness of Arab Christian literature. Louis Massignon gave many talks there. The Dar as-Salam provided a sanctuary for Islamic/Christian dialogue through an organization formed by Father Ayrout and some Islamic professors in 1941 called Ikhwan as-Safa, The Sincere Brothers.

In 1936 Massignon had become friends with Monsignor Montini, a Cardinal whose work in the Vatican moved him from being the deputy to the future Pius Xll to eventually being elected himself as Pope Paul Vl. Mary Kahil's friendship with the Greek Catholic auxiliary Bishop, Kamel Medawar, led to the official approval by the Church for the Badaliya on January 6, 1947 and Monsignor Montini became a member. Mary and Massignon gave Bishop Medawar a written copy of the statutes agreed to by the members describing their daily efforts to live in the spirit of Badaliya.

They agreed to pray for the Muslims, to treat them with respect, affection and kindness, and to personally live the gospel message of love in their daily lives. Like Mary they devoted themselves to the Muslim community by volunteering in organizations where they could live out the spirit intended by the Badaliya. They met once a week for an hour. Guided by his relationship with Charles de Foucauld Massignon invited them to begin their gatherings with a silent prayer before the altar called "adoration." Then they read the spiritual writings of Foucauld or others, and ended with praying together. From 1947 to the end of his life Massignon wrote a letter every year to the members of the Badaliya in Cairo expressing the intensity of his spiritual vocation and the profound mystery of mystical substitution.

On February 5th, 1949 Massignon received the permission of Pope Pius Xll to change his affiliation with the Latin church in order to worship as a member of the Greek Catholic Melkite Church. Now he was able to worship in solidarity with his Arab Christian brothers and sisters as one of them. With Mary's help and encouragement he began to pursue his dream of ordination to the priesthood. In a private celebration witnessed by Mary Kahil at Our Lady of Peace, Massignon was ordained a Greek Catholic Melkite priest by Bishop Medawar on January 28, 1950.

The Sacrifice

In his letters to Mary, Massignon often referred to his inner spiritual journey with images of being cast out to sea on a small boat, a bark or barge, sometimes drowning in the waves or floating on a calmer ocean, rising and falling with the tide. In this way he spoke of his overwhelming desire for God using the images of his spiritual guide, al-Hallaj.[15] From childhood he had spent every summer of his life on the coast of France in Brittany which surely reinforced his meditation. In 1951, after many years of sharing their spiritual experiences, Massignon asked Mary to enter into a fast of silence with him by agreeing not to write very often nor see one another. He wrote, "If you have climbed into my bark it was so that I could lead you to the open sea, beyond any visible coast, in order for you to get off there. Have confidence in the grace of God; write to me to speak to me of Him, the Lover for whom we wish to live and die...."[16]

Massignon was inviting Mary to join him in a difficult and painful test of faith in the ability of God's love to bind us to one another through the sacrifice of Jesus. He was teaching her how to truly give herself entirely to God, and to trust that God's love had always been her guide and would be forever. In order that the Badaliya truly bear fruit they must experience this sacrifice of themselves, to wholly lose themselves in mystical substitution for those for whom they prayed. Mary was suddenly left in solitude and silence. In the beginning it was a terrible trial for her that she understood was demanded of her by God. She knew that Massignon was there, praying with her and for her and leading the way towards Jesus, yet she struggled to finally come to thanking God for allowing her to experience the annihilation of herself in Christ. In her journal she wrote, "that there is no more of me than a little bit of ashes."[17]

Mary continued with her activities in Cairo. The creation of the state of Israel in 1948 and the encouragement of Egyptian nationalism in 1956 by Nassar led to discrimination of foreigners and minorities. Many Syro-Lebanese families emigrated to the United States and Canada. Mary's property in Damietta was confiscated. By 1959 she and Massignon had begun to see one another and to write again but she knew that they were both getting older and that if they did see one another it would be one of the last times. On October 31, 1962 Louis Massignon died in Paris at the age of 79.

Massignon had written to Mary about his concern for the continuation of the Badaliya. Now she would truly go on without him. In her journal Mary speaks both to herself and to God in her prayer, "Well now, from this day on, it is necessary that I stay alone, alone with You, O my God. I think I wish to stay alone in this cell which is my own world. I need Your Grace, O my God. But everything is grace, because there is complete strength in me. Give your worries back to God, Mary, let's hope that you give me all your thoughts and preoccupations. Be mine alone."[18]

The Sincere Brothers organization was dissolved under Nassar's regime and recreated by Mary and the former minister of Health, Doctor Abdo Essallam in 1975. By then Mary was in her 80's. Meetings were held every three weeks at Dar as-Salam. In a peaceful and welcoming atmosphere Christians and Muslims came together to present their different points of view and try to understand one another better. Each meeting closed with a prayer recited together in Arabic:

"We come to you together with our hearts filled with good will and respect. We beg you to grant us constant support. May your light, which guides us on straight paths, make us sincere in the adoration we give to you, that we are counselled and guided by those sent by you and by your prophets, and that we bring about what pleases you, while each of us stay loyal to our faith and religion, love our neighbors, and always go forward on the way to progress and success."[19]

Part Three: Spiritual Reflections by Mary Kahil

From the beginning Mary worked towards social justice especially for Egyptian women. Throughout her life she remained an active Christian dedicated to her Greek Catholic Melkite tradition. Through the available fragments from letters to Louis Massignon and Mary's personal journals we can see the effect of her relationship with him on her growing spirituality. The Dar as-Salam provided a place for integrating that spirituality with social action, education and increased awareness as well as providing a forum for Muslim/Christian dialogue. Mary found the spiritual foundation for her social consciousness inspired by Massignon. His spiritual journey also led him ever more passionately towards social action as the political situation intensified between France, and Morocco and Algeria.

The Badaliya became the focal point of an inner spiritual journey rooted and shaped by their passionate offering of themselves to God for others. They were substitutes in Huysmans' long line of saints, chosen through the ages to give their lives for the salvation of all of us, which began with the sacrifice of Jesus on the cross. The Badaliya inevitably nurtured the desire for social justice as well. Massignon's insight was profoundly Christian yet equally grounded in all three Abrahamic religions as he perceived them; there was Abraham's willingness to sacrifice his son, Isaac, Jesus' death on a cross, and al-Hallaj's martyrdom for the sake of unity in the Muslim community. Yet the Badaliya was primarily inspired by a deep and overpowering love and longing for God that can only be called "mystical."

Badaliya:

Mary's reflections in this section on her relationship with Louis Massignon and her own spirituality are taken from the fragmented portions of her journal and a few letters that still exist.

In 1935 when Mary and Massignon had just begun their annual ritual of renewing their vows of Badaliya, she hardly understood what Massignon was inviting her to experience. She wrote: "He often had tears in his eyes, so profound, and I could not understand. It was too heavy for me to understand, to believe in his unreasonable love."[20]

Mary and Massignon repeated their vows of Badaliya by making pilgrimages every year to different sacred places. They found ancient, deserted and hidden churches and chapels dedicated to various saints and prophets. Mary wrote:

> "We went with great faith up above Carmel. Going through the brambles and cork-oaks which invaded the trail. Wild vegetation, steep landscapes, the sea all the way down in the distance. We find an old church, open, deserted. Saint Elijah cutting the throats of the priests of Baal. In naked faith we remake our vows of Badaliya."[21]

Of visits to the Litostrothos Haifa, and Mary of Jesus Crucified, Mary wrote:

> "Lying prostrate, sinking onto the stone, he, burning with fever, bleeding with emotion, me, deaf and blind, prostrate at the feet of the Lord, on these stones touched by his footprints."

> "At Haifa, we went to the Carmelite church in the grotto of Saint Elijah. Thunderstorm outside. The waves furiously beating against the sides of the mountain. But there we made the offering of ourselves for Islam and remade our vows. I spent the night at "Stella Maris," all alone, dying of fright at the fury of the waves."

> "Marie Bawouardi, Carmelite. We went up a pretty steep slope to get to this village. We pray to the young saint with faith in our Badaliya which was the indisolvable tie of our spiritual union. He had a blind faith in every sign of God."[22]

The Priest:

On February 1, 1950 Mary, who calls herself by her Arabic name, Maryam, wrote a letter to Massignon who had just been ordained as a Melkite Priest. For the first time she addressed her friend and mentor as Father.

"My Father, I participated in your Sacrifice, I received the holy Body of Jesus Christ and His precious Blood from your sacred hands; at night, I think of your preparation, by day your offering. Everything in life is changed for me and a new way opens itself for Maryam if she is faithful to the inner call to solitude and to the presence of the interior Guest. It seems to me that this one who has unchanging plans for us is saying something to me and as I have no way to reflect alone, I will put myself in his presence by writing to you and in my journal with this inner opening to his voice, which is silence. You said that only the virginal word can penetrate into the intimate sanctuary of the soul and provoke this tacit acceptance of the *Fiat*, [the Virgin Mary's Yes to God] which is the conception of Christ in us. Also, I will retire often into my inner room, there where he deigns to wait for me. I will show him my mother's room, the one who gave me life. Oh! My friend, it is so beautiful, and all that is beautiful. And I believe it and walk there on the clouds, like in a waking dream!"[23]

Mary calls Massignon by his Franciscan name in Arabic, Ibrahim. On February 9, 1950, on the anniversary of their shared vows of Badaliya, she wrote:

"I want to consecrate myself to Him too, with Ibrahim, and I want to live His presence in me every morning at your sacrifice [Mass]. To unite myself there as an offering, a victim of merciful love, like Thérèse, and to remember it many times a day...."[24]

Alone with God:

Massignon first taught Mary to rely on God alone in 1951. He asked her to join him in following the early Christian and Islamic understanding of fasting as including a vow of silence. It was a Catholic tradition to make this vow one week before the Feast of the Assumption of Mary, on August 15th, in order to permit the Word of God to be conceived in her and in us. We must pay the price, which is silence, in order to hear that Word and join the young Virgin Mary in her *Fiat*, her "Yes" to God. Massignon wrote that the *Fiat* is the beginning of all mysticism.[25] For Mary Kahil the price was a painful trial that took several years for her to finally write these words in her journal:

> "I would like to live another life in order to thank God enough, which isn't possible, for annihilating me more in Christ so that there is no more of me than a small amount of ashes."[26]

On August 15, 1964 Mary remembered that time of separation from one another, and the letter from Massignon that pronounced it, in what she called her "verdict" and he later called her "novitiate":

> "In this week so poignant for me, at the feet of my Lord and Master, I relived this period, 15 years: 1951 when I received via Rossi the fateful letter with my verdict. I bless Jesus for this wound which tore my heart open, but which set my path and my life. Oh, my God, enlighten me even if I am not worthy. Oh, Lord, teach me your justice. Come Holy Spirit."[27]

Mary and Massignon resumed communication and in 1960 he wrote that perhaps they were near to their last days and letters. Although she admitted her feelings of despair she wrote:

> "....The Lord is more beautiful and generous than I would have ever known to imagine, Ibrahim. My heart bursts with gratitude, with unhoped for renewal.... And here before the altar where you were consecrated I renew this infinite surge towards the heart of the Master of our lives, delivering to Him that which still

remains to burn in me, the rest of this heart which must burn with love until it dies of it. Because we don't accept apathy or mediocrity, nor the spiritual sleep of our time, we go to Him in the fire of love which He lights in our hearts. It is for this that I wish to stay lucid. May He always grace us with it. It is this light which lit up your letter of December 8, on this feast of the Immaculate which left me a perfume of lilies and incense in the memory of the heart.

"It is on this blessed day that the Holy Virgin inspired you to write to me and to make this nightmare which crushed me vanish, having believed I offended you in order to merit this verdict of exclusion, like Hagar in the desert long ago. I spend my time doing actions of grace, of renewal, stammering spontaneous psalms to the Lord for having given back my hope to die in your good graces and friendship. My brother, prostrated in adoration, continue the will of God, whatever that may be."[28]

Mary's Journey: The Cross and the Resurrection

On October 31, 1962 the eve of All Saints Day, Louis Massignon died. Mary wrote that Jesus had planted her love for Massignon in her heart like a cross, because God is love. On November 31, 1962, one month after his death, Mary wrote in her journal:

"....He won't be mentioned with all the other saints. He will be a saint all alone, he will be a saint. And me, I sailed in bitter waters, sinking into mud up to my neck. I splashed about in the mire, because the sadness, and even despair, bewitched me in their obscure shadow. Then I went back to the small Franciscan chapel that he loved so much. Before the nativity scene, roses before the infant Jesus, and there I suffered so much.... Now I took my cross on my shoulders and I made my way of the cross with it and I understood at the 14th station that the tomb of Jesus was my heart, since through the Holy Presence I keep him in this tomb from which he will be gloriously resurrected.

Louis always wrote to me of the resurrection. He knew that he was going to die, and I didn't know, and I hold Jesus lovingly, dead, but living in me through the Holy Presence in this heart-tomb. Jesus, lovingly held by me, in me, that Massignon's love gave to me.

And I didn't know. And the night before his death, of his passing, I saw him in black, reassuring me, passing by like a shadow, flying past like a star, and sadly I savored this vision.

In the morning I arrange to go to Damietta, instinctively, blindly. I cannot sleep all night. It passed, it passed. He called me to Damietta. To receive his soul, there where he had wished to die. In this decayed church...."[29]

Desire for God:

As the years went by after Massignon's death, Mary struggled to grow in her faith. On January 5, 1963, the Feast of the Epiphany, Mary went on a pilgrimage to a Carmelite church where Massignon had celebrated Mass. She wrote this prayer in memory of her friend:

> "I came on a pilgrimage to say to you, Oh Jesus, that you are our spouse, our beloved, our only friend, and I ask to love you with all this poor heart, emptied and extinguished, now that I am all alone before you. Accept me, so poor, and in my last hour accept me as I am, poor and extinguished before you."[30]

On July 22, 1964 Mary prayed to Mary Magdalene:

"Mary chose her part... And you, Maryam? While there is still time, choose to live the end of your life at his feet. I want to tell you my prayer, not by those commanded, stereotyped or organized by and for everyone. A very little prayer like that of the bird who sang this morning on the white poplar. He spoke his love. I would like to tell you of my love, my closed up love, imprisoned, enslaved, stuck, in misery, in dust. This chain on my neck, this millstone around my neck, that I pull on the gravel, this stony route of life, with pain, with anguish, with such powerlessness, with this helpless love and useless distress. Praying for them, suffering for them, loving all of them. With your grace I want to love....."[31]

Running from God:

Mary returned to Lebanon in September 1964 struggling to find her way:

"Here is the place of my rest, in my childhood surroundings which awakens in me beauty and poetry, because each pine tree is deeply rooted in my heart, every spring runs through me. There is such eloquence in this suggestive silence. All these trees speak to me without stopping of the one who travelled up and down these mountains. Oh, my heart's sadness, I who don't know how to love. Oh, drama of my life, I who don't know how to listen, to listen to the inner voice, the silent and continuing call, the call of one who I don't listen to. Oh fatal, frenzied journey, towards whom, towards what? Oh Maryam, unsatisfied, incomplete, fool racing on the highways of the world, tell me when you will rest, when will you stop running, blind and enraged, towards whom, towards what? Where is your life?

Oh my God, if I don't know how to thank you, forgive me, if I don't know how to understand, excuse me. If I don't know how to come, pull me. Oh my God, my only concern, my only preoccupation. Oh Jesus my only interest in this life and in the next. My only anguish, to not wait for you. My only sorrow to not love you enough."[32]

Finding her God:

On July 21, 1965 in Salzburg Mary wrote:

"And now on this solemn and grave day for me, I understand that it is necessary to enter into solitude, silently and to be a believer.... I believe in God almighty and eternal, who creates his kingdom in souls, I believe and am convinced that you create your kingdom in me. This special kingdom, started by Massignon...

I must stay enclosed in this tent, this interior life that I looked for mechanically all my life, but which I did not have the courage to build, nor to introduce myself to, nor to watch over, I was so attracted to the outside, to contacts, success, self-assurance, the glow of the footlights....

And now, from this day on, I must stay alone, alone with you, Oh my God..... This morning I thought again of the Mass in the little chapel at Saint Mary of Peace, her ornaments, in crepe, torn, but embroidered in pure gold, crumpled. Have pity on me, I am a sinner. That Christ be with us into eternity, he said to me, turning toward me. He named me the first in his consecration of the Body and the Blood of the Lord. And me, I am like a napping animal, without thought or feeling. Now I alone must pray for him, and in his place because he has given back to me alone the care of his soul and his salvation. If I was not worthy of it, it is necessary to begin now to fast, to pray, to fill this role he can no longer fill, being for him in the hereafter, in Badaliya in his place, as we thought to do the first days of our joyful union. Believe, Mary, that it is Jesus so tender and so good who sent him to you. Believe in the love in this heart which loved you, without your wanting to believe him. You are an ingracious fool to not notice, to respond to this infinite call, the call of your God, of your spouse. Oh Jesus, open my icy heart."[33]

In a letter written from Cairo on November 29, 1970, at the age of 81, Mary wrote to her friend, the writer, Yvonne Chauffin. Mary reflects Massignon's great desire to see Jerusalem as a free city open to all religious pilgrims. True to Massignon's "communion of saints" she asks for his intervention.

"I hoped to meet you—and to speak of all the things unexpressed; to find again a little of the atmosphere of our great departed friend; and also, they sent me the Cahier de L'Herne where Massignon is so admirably evoked and refound! I have had a superhuman joy; I read it like a catechism, with devotion; but I did not find your name there, dear Yvonne, you who knew and admired him so much. Do you dare to write something in memory of him? How much I would love to read and savor it!

Me, I continue to live, to understand and to feel my limits in every relationship. I am interested with all my heart in the cause of Palestine which is my mental homeland; and I hope that Massignon will obtain for us the liberation of Jerusalem."[34]

Mary Kahil died in 1979 at the age of 90.
When Massignon received permission to become a worshipping member of the Greek Catholic Melkite Church he fulfilled part of his vow to offer himself to God as a substitute

for the Arab people and Islam. At the moment of his conversion he had made his first desperate prayer to God for help in Arabic. For Massignon, who was so drawn to the symbolic meaning and sources of language, Arabic was the language of prayer. Now he was able to completely live his vocation of Badaliya and it was also one more step towards his unfulfilled desire to become a priest. In the Greek Catholic Melkite tradition married men were accepted into the priesthood.

When Maximos IV was elected as Patriarch of the Greek Catholic Melkite Church in 1947 Mary Kahil and Massignon began to speak with Bishop Medawar about the possibility of ordination. Massignon was introduced to the role of the priest by Charles de Foucauld who intensely experienced the self-sacrifice of Jesus in the Eucharistic ritual performed by Catholic priests in the Mass. For Massignon this was the ultimate expression of Badaliya, and for this reason, throughout his life, the priesthood was his deepest desire. When he spoke with Maximos IV it was his vow to offer his life in Badaliya, mystical substitution, for his Muslim brothers and sisters that convinced the Patriarch to approve his request to become a Melkite priest. Like the personal and deeply spiritual vow of mystical substitution for the Muslim community, Massignon's vow to the priesthood was lived out by celebrating the Mass in Arabic every day in private. He was not called to be a public minister but rather a hidden mystical substitute for others. His ordination, which was controversial in Rome and not easily understood by his own family, took place on January 28, 1950, one day before the sixteenth anniversary of his renewed relationship with Mary Kahil in 1934. And it was she who arranged and paid for Bishop Medawar to come from Damascus when Massignon wrote to her of his plan to be in Cairo and of his desire to fulfill his dream of ordination to the priesthood at that time.

It was almost as though Massignon's death in 1962 had a prophetic meaning after he exhausted himself on behalf of the Muslim and Arab people. Perhaps his lifetime of love for God and prayer of substitution for his Muslim friends was about to bear fruit, and his God called him home. Surely as a member of the Badaliya, Monsignor Montini, who was now Pope Paul VI, was profoundly influenced by his longtime friend Louis Massignon. He called the Bishops from all over the world to gather in Rome for the second session of the Vatican ll Council held from 1962 to 1965. The documents they wrote concerning people of other faith traditions, especially our Jewish and Muslim brothers and sisters, were revolutionary. The Badaliya and the Dar as-Salam were a spark that finally caught fire.

Chapter Six

Two Prayers From The Heart
Christine the Admirable and Joan of Arc

ALTHOUGH THIS IS A BOOK about those saints and mystics who influenced Louis Massignon's unique spirituality, it is inevitable that he himself would in turn become a guiding force for others. Just as he was a mentor for Mary Kahil, many others also experienced him as a spiritual guide through his years of correspondence by letters, his published and unpublished articles and lectures, volumes of books, and through their relationships with him as students and friends. His reputation as an erudite scholar seemed to contradict his equally intense personal pursuit of his spiritual calling. It is in his four-volume *Passion of al-Hallaj* and his writings about the saints, and prayers to them, that we discover the depth of his spirituality.

In an essay written in 1950 about Christine the Admirable, Massignon reminds us that the great architectural monuments and cathedrals arising out of a flourishing Christianity in the Middle Ages would one day collapse and erode with the passage of time. He suggests that there are works of holiness that are far more worthy of our attachment, and which never perish. These are the "sacred souls, true invisible cathedrals" who offered themselves in compassion to God, taking on all the misery of suffering humanity, uniting themselves, and all of us, to Christ. He calls the life of these saints "music sung in many voices," yet he writes that those biographers who wish to repeat their melodies for us have not always had the necessary "impeccable throat, breath or tone." Here he apologizes for his unworthiness as he begins his own essay about Saint Christine the Admirable. Like Huysmans' biography of Saint Lydwine before him, Massignon's reflections on this 13th century mystic offer us an understanding of his own spirituality. It points to the sources for his own vow of Badaliya, which was a silent invitation to every Christian by the first substitute, Christ himself.

Part One: Christine the Admirable[1]

Christine's story begins in the city of Liège, Belgium, which saw an important movement towards Christian renewal at the beginning of the 13th century. This renewal caused an increase in scholars and even addressed the education of women. It was influenced by the flourishing of monasteries where both men and women sought and achieved holiness. The same historian who witnessed and carefully documented the life of Francis of Assisi in 1216 also knew Christine and wrote about what he observed of her life. Jacques de Vitry wrote a letter about her to his friend, Bishop Foulques of Toulouse in which Massignon discovered what he considered to be the decisive historic text concerning Saint Christine. What we can say with certainty is that she was born in Brusthem, near to St. Trond in 1150. She lived in St. Trond, Liège and in Looz. She died in 1224. Jacques de Vitry begins his letter with his admiration for the "silent fervor" of the virgins, widows and married country women in the South of France who originally came from Liège.

He tells us that he personally knew another holy woman named Christine who, much like Saint Lydwine, was compelled by God to atone for the sins of humanity by experiencing extraordinary tortures, such as rolling on burning embers and plunging into ice water in the middle of the winter. She even climbed onto the gibbet to pray and suffer at the side of an already executed criminal, associating herself with his damnation and physical tortures. Once her penance was achieved she lived in peace and received many graces from God. She so delighted in the spirit that she was able to guide other souls to the threshold of purgatory, even making them go through it without wounding themselves in their efforts to reach the supreme kingdom. He also describes a miracle that he attributes to God. After having been dead for some time and lying in her coffin before being put in the earth, Christine was said to have revived, her soul returning to her body.

Whether these miracles are true or false, Massignon suggests that they remain a part of human history. They affect us like the biblical stories of the miracles of Jesus, or the stories found in the Middle East of the dances and songs of jubilation by lovers of God condemned to die, like al-Hallaj. He writes: "In fact, at the time of a miracle, the saints, who are passive instruments, confess their powerlessness. Their will unites itself so well with the divine will that it is consumed like a burning straw." Only those who participate in the kind of submission to God that Christ did can experience the same exaltation and Ascension that He did. Only those souls who recognize the holiness of God, or experience it in the transparency of another sacred soul, seem to be prepared to accept miracles as paths towards the Divine.

> "The miracle itself is the pretext, the point of insertion of a conversion. Since it is visible, it inserts in us the delight of loving invisible realities. And this is the important point: The conversion of heart and the divine forgiveness which follows, finds itself thus sealed, provoked by the felt miracle. Weak men and fragile women have accepted and practiced a severe rule of life, renouncing everything until death because one day, suddenly, they were surprised by supernatural phenomena."[2]

Perhaps it was while someone preached or spoke about a miracle that they suddenly knew in whom they believed. Massignon suggests that this is what happened to Jacques de

Vitry and this is why he gives such weight to his testimony about Christine the Admirable.

Jacques de Vitry was an intelligent and active student who was pursuing a career as a preacher and theologian but did not make particularly rigorous demands on himself as a Christian. He was keenly interested in the power that stems from knowledge, and this is what sparked his curiosity about these poor, illiterate, and reclusive women who suffered atrocious afflictions yet were said to be divinely inspired. Seeking them out was not a very pleasant idea since he expected to be confronted with trivia and sentimentalities. Instead their pure and direct gaze caused him to suddenly feel judged, his heart probed to reveal his most perplexing secrets. Near to them he suddenly felt himself become a different person. Massignon wrote:

> "Many of us have had this experience when blessed with meeting such simple and pure souls before whom we blush to have a bad thought. Afterwards we want to get hold of ourselves by saying that it was an illusion, that our imagination has forged an unrealistic idol of purity for us. But no. With one simple word or silent look we once again find ourselves seen through, without being betrayed, by the angelic smile of an incorruptible witness, reminding us with a tearing intensity of all our promises to love God, and scorning these tokens of our weakness."

Jacques de Vitry learned the mystical sense of the history of humanity from them and understood the meaning of Jesus' sacrifice. From century to century God arouses men and women like Christine and Francis who agree to carry the sins of the world. They thereby give Jesus the joy of suffering again through them for us, thus perfecting His passion. This was the foundation of Massignon's own spirituality nurtured by his connections to Huysmans and Charles de Foucauld. It inspired his passion for researching the sources for the life stories of the saints, like Christine, who form a silent chain of mystical substitutes through the centuries.

Massignon wonders if Christine the Admirable could glorify God any better, or love and serve others better than to endure for them what Jesus endured. Christine was the first and the most astonishing example of this vocation to live a secret life of penitence in the 13th century. It isn't necessary to be a cloistered religious, nor even a woman, but rather to offer ourselves to God without ceasing so that Jesus can offer Himself to us, and for us, without ceasing. Massignon calls this vocation a "triumph of humility." If we are the church, then the construction of the church will only be accomplished by our own inner compassion, consuming desire, and our heroic acceptance of the cross.

Massignon made two pilgrimages to Liège, one in September 1912, and one in July 1924. At the age of 41 he was able to see how his spiritual path had deep roots in his earliest memories and how those reminded him of painful losses in his life. For thirteen years he had written faithfully every week to his friend Luis de Cuadra and continued to pray for his return to Christianity. On August 12, 1921 Luis de Cuadra committed suicide. Some months later, in January 1922 Massignon wrote to Luis de Cuadra's father to find out more information about his friend's death. On January 16th he received a letter informing him that Luis' father had also committed suicide. The very next day, January 18, 1922, Massignon's own father, Pierre Roche died while in the midst of sculpting a bust of his friend J.-K. Huysmans in his studio. The pain of the loss of these two important people in his life was compounded by his anguish for the souls of both of them. He did not know if his prayers for his friend had reconciled him to God and he knew that his father had not received the sacraments before his death. Now, two years later, in 1924, while writing about the 13th century mystic, Christine the Admirable, he was reminded of an engraving of her that his father had sketched in 1902 at the request of J.-K. Huysmans. At the end of his essay he wrote this prayer for his father:

"I wish in ending to recall my first meeting with Christine the Admirable. It was 20 years ago, towards my 20th year, very far from the faith of my childhood. Among all the effigies of beauty, profane and profaned, tempting or suspect, which presented themselves at the door of my imagination in meeting works of art, suddenly this image appeared, adorned in singular glory, the glory of holiness.

It was a simple engraving in relief sketched in 1902 by a sculptor at the instigation of J.-K. Huysmans, the author of Saint Lydwine. One could see it high up, Christine, her hands joined, praying in ecstacy, perched like a bird on the highest beam of a gallows, while the tortured, for whom she interceded were heavily weighted down by their twisted cadavers on the hooks of the hinges at the bottom, under the misty sun. The antithesis of innocence and of crime, a confrontation with despair and prayer, an imperious call to a meditation on death.

It is now 20 years later. This engraving is now in my home, seen every day when I pray, the thought of death presenting itself like a knife. It reminds me again of hopeless confidences by many encountering the threshold of agony, of earlier happy friends who finally committed suicide, while by an unexpected intervention, God remade me Christian. Jesus is there, vigilant in this image of Saint Christine making us believe that nothing is impossible with love, that prayer can dare anything, that it will lift our souls to God forever, outside of the dungeon of our sins, the tombs of our failed good resolutions, the perjury in our sermons, and our betrayed vows.

The artist who conceived this humble engraving died 2 years ago without having the time to reconcile himself with the Church sacramentally. It is for him, for his soul, fulfilling a strict duty, that I ask here, respectfully and humbly, for the alms and prayers of the Church, by all of you, through the intercession of Christine the Admirable before God." [3]

Part Two: Saint Joan of Arc

"Si Bermont fut le lieu de sa vocation, Chînon fut celui de son destin."
(If she found her vocation in Bermont, Chînon was where she found her destiny.")
—Louis Massignon

Saint Joan was important to Louis Massignon's father, Ferdinand, a sculptor well known in France as Pierre Roche. His grandparents were peasants from an area of France that lies between the rivers Oise and Yerre, called Vexin. Despite his education in medicine and the arts, and intellectual resistance to a belief in God, Pierre Roche experienced a sense of mystery hidden in nature and remained susceptible to thoughts of the simple agricultural life of his ancestors. In 1889 he made a private pilgrimage to Domremy. He was drawn to the birthplace of Joan of Arc in recognition of her astounding role in restoring French unity in the fifteenth century. He perceived her as giving birth to France.[4]

He must have known of Joan's pending case for canonization begun in 1869. She was once again the subject of a trial in a process that ultimately took fifty years to complete. I wonder what blessing this artist was seeking on his pilgrimage to the virgin of Domremy? Perhaps a blessing for the tools of his work as an artist. His son, Louis, was influenced from childhood by his father's creative work and always remembered the artistic impression of Joan of Arc, a medallion, that sat on his father's studio table.

Louis Massignon's conversion experience in Iraq in 1908 became a source of tension between Louis and his father. It was difficult for Ferdinand Massignon to understand his son's experience. It seems that their shared affection for Saint Joan became the avenue to healing their differences. On April 18, 1909, the day that Joan of Arc was beatified in Rome, Louis and his father went to Domremy on a pilgrimage together to thank the maid of Orleans for their reconciliation.

Her Life

There was an aura of mystery in France in the fifteenth century that seems to elude us today in our computerized age of scientific discovery and ever-increasing technology. Then, there was an intuitive sense of a mythic dimension to life. Angels and saints, the supernatural, felt intertwined in the everyday, accessible through prayer and devotion. Myth, legend and prophecy gave hope in the face of the harsh realities of the Hundred Years War, the threat to national identity, and the added pressure of civil war.

There were rumors of an ancient prophecy that some said dated back to the time of King Arthur's Merlin. It claimed, "a young virgin would come from the oak forest in the marshes of Lorraine to do marvellous acts and save France."[5] In the woods near the village of Greux, not far from Domremy, there is a small chapel called Our Lady of Bermont which once belonged to a hermitage. Young girls came there to light candles and pray to the wooden statue of the Virgin Mary. Among them was a serious and, some say, too pious child who was born in Domremy into a peasant family around 1412. She was destined to become a legendary figure, known to the world as a saint, prophetess and martyr, and revered as a national heroine.

In the French city of Rouen in 1431, nineteen-year-old Joan of Arc, known as Jeanne la Pucelle in France, was burned at the stake, condemned of heresy by her church, and sorcery by her civil executioners. Just twenty years later she was cleared of wrong-doing by a rehabilitation process begun primarily for political reasons by Charles VII. As the result of the military efforts of his army, led by the maid of Domremy, he was crowned

King of France at Reims in 1429, going on to reclaim French national unity after Joan's untimely death.

A cloud of mystery and controversy surrounded Joan's mission, as well as her courage as a young woman in medieval times called to lead an army to victory. She claimed to hear the voices of Saints who urged her to approach the disinherited dauphin at Chînon, to inform him of her mission and ask for arms and men to reclaim the cities and villages on the way to Reims and his rightful crown. Joan prayed and listened, convinced of God's call to her. She was born to this and knew that her God would show her the way. Her passion, conviction, and her voices and piety, along with her achievements in two short years, planted the seeds of legend and a heroine was born.

Joan's story gave birth to volumes of artistic expression and has been the inspiration for almost six centuries of poems, plays, operas, films, sculptures and paintings. Her legend and its controversies continued to coax the imagination into the mid eighteen hundreds when the historical Joan first appeared in Jean Michelet's *History of France*, and then in Jules Quicherat's five volumes of the complete texts of the trial and rehabilitation process. Despite those and more current psychological efforts to explain or interpret her life, her voices and the success of her mission remain unique and mysterious to this day. Joan was canonized by the Roman Catholic Church in 1920 and honored by George Bernard Shaw in his great play *Saint Joan* which was later made into a film, recently restored. We continue to be touched by her, to write poems and direct our prayers to her as her story continues to be retold and new films created.

I fell in love with Joan of Arc when I saw the 1948 film starring Ingrid Bergman. I was left with an impression of a holy woman who loved God above all else. She seemed to me to be earthy, human, and real, alive with passion and love. At the same time she became my role model for devotion and my glimpse of the divine. I was only eight years old. Something in me resonated with this illiterate peasant girl whose loyalty to her country and her God led her into a fierce battle against injustice. Villages in France were burned to the ground and the peasants governed by what Joan perceived as foreign power. She put on armor, raised the banner dedicated to her Lord Jesus and the Virgin Mary and miraculously became a military leader. I was in awe of her courage but also her faith and trust in God.

Massignon calls Joan of Arc an "artistic paradox of inviolate virginity." He suggests the irony of imagining a virgin invested with the power to give birth to life as Joan did to France. This is a theme found throughout Massignon's writing as he probes the layers of meaning attributed to the Virgin Mary by generations of Christians and Muslims, and finds correspondences in great women through the centuries. Like Joan, Mary too was said to hear messages from God that determined her vocation and ultimately her place of reverence in both religions.

When I was a teenager in Europe I remember being ushered reluctantly from one historic church to another by my mother. Her passion for sacred art and the spectacular stained glass representations of biblical scenes has become one of my fondest memories of her. I am still drawn to them and find myself caught up in the mystery of the Annunciation scenes where Mary, still a child herself, gazes with innocence and wonder as a heavenly figure announces her destiny. Generations continue to pray for her intercession, granting her the power to bless the tools of our labor, to give birth to life, bear healthy children, and make our fields fertile. We turn to the "inviolate virgin" paradoxically as a symbol of fertility, perhaps yet unaware that it is the inviolate core of ourselves that gives birth to fruitfulness in our world. I too gaze with innocence and wonder at this mystery, revealed ever more brilliantly when shafts of sunlight stream into the cool darkness of stone churches through colorful stained glass windows.

There is more to the "artistic paradox" that Massignon identifies with Joan of Arc because she carried a sword as she urged her soldiers on in battle, which he calls "a sword of all sparkling fire." This is the famous sword found at Fierbois that Joan mysteriously knew was buried in the church of Saint

Catherine behind the altar. It was engraved with five crosses and was said to have shone brilliantly when the rust miraculously fell away. Joan's prosecutors skillfully avoided much emphasis on this miracle for fear that it demonstrated proof of her faithful devotion to her God and her ultimate innocence. Her sword, like that often seen in representations of Saint Paul, was a symbol, according to Massignon, of "angelic nakedness." It was a sparkling paradox of spiritual meaning for Joan, rather than an instrument of destruction, for even in battle she piously refused to kill her enemies, purposely holding her banner high instead of her sword. Thus she revealed her angelic witness to the power of Transcendent Mystery, leaving her naked and unarmed in the midst of battle.

I am reminded of an immense stained glass window of Saint Paul with a Bible in one hand and a prominent silver sword in the other rising above the altar in a nearby chapel. I went there recently to hear a talk on Black history in America and the future of Democracy, and could not avoid the challenge in that gleaming silver sword. "Draw your strength from the Lord and his mighty power.—Take the helmet of salvation and the sword of the spirit, the word of God."[6] I remembered how Charles de Gaulle honored Jeanne la Pucelle by making the cross of Lorraine the emblem of free France during World War ll, and yet Joan knew that the Word of God is the true sword of the spirit leading to real freedom. Within the same century we in America have yet to honor the sword of Christ that the prophet Simeon states will pierce Mary's soul so that "the thoughts of many hearts will be laid bare."[7] It is a two-edged sword that insists that we overcome our deep fear of the Blacks, Hispanic and Asians who live in our own neighborhoods and risk piercing the heart of our prejudices with the Love of God, vision of equality, and basic human rights that once created our brave new nation. We still struggle to give birth to these ideals, laboring on the sharp edge of pain and suffering, battling against racism, sexism and exploitation in order to one day hold the sword of God's all sparkling fire and love with Joan of Arc. Can we also finally vow to kill no other human being and compassionately hear the confessions of our enemies as they lie dying in our arms as Joan did, praying that they too would share her Heaven?

They captured Joan and put her on trial much as the Islamic mystic al-Hallaj was imprisoned and finally condemned as a heretic in 922 CE. Hallaj was crucified and dismembered and Joan was burned at the stake five hundred years later. Both were martyrs to their faith and their dying once again gave birth to the power of myth to transcend culture and history by pointing to Transcendent Mystery. They were both caught in the web of intrigue and suspicion created by the controversy between orthodox institutional tradition and individual inspiration. Hallaj is said to have danced in his chains as they led him to the gibbet, ecstatic with devotion. He once cried out: "O people! When *Haqq* (God) takes possession of a heart, He empties it of all but Himself; and when He keeps a man for Himself, He ruins him for all but Himself. When He lovingly desires a servant, He incites His other servants to enmity against him, so as to bring him closer to Himself."[8]

Joan's heart too was possessed by her God. In her long and arduous trial she was subject to every trick of interrogation and yet managed to remain clear, focused, and direct in her responses. Her memory for detail was remarkable despite her lack of education and illiteracy. She was asked by the institutional Church to denounce her voices and betray her vocation. She replied: "I call this impossible—that I should revoke the things that I have said and done, as they are set down in this trial, concerning the visions and revelations which I have said that I had from God. Not for anything will I revoke them. And what our Lord has caused and commanded me to do, and shall command, I will not cease from doing for any man living.—And in case the Church wished to make me do something else, contrary to the commandment which I say God has given me, not for anything would I do it."[9]

As I sat half listening to the speaker, the image of Saint Paul momentarily became Joan with her banner raised high, her sword shimmering as the last rays of the setting sun streamed through the stained glass. When the lecturer invited this young audience of students to voice their dreams for the future of my country, I thought of Joan and Hallaj. These witnesses to an integrity of belief in the face of social injustice and terrifying personal consequences wound my selfish heart. They provoke me to wake up, not only to the uncertain future of democracy in America but to the impossibility of a global realization of mutuality and community if we cannot respond to the call of Love, like Hallaj and Joan responded, with compassion and unwavering devotion to God and all of humanity. Each of them was called to social action out of the depth of their prayer and stand for us as witnesses to the continuing movement of the Spirit in the world. Social action must find its courage and vision grounded in prayer and passionate love.

Part Three: Massignon's Prayer to Saint Joan

Louis Massignon drew a lifetime of inspiration for research and prayer as well as social action from these legendary figures. In the last eight years of his life he took up his own "sword of all sparkling fire." Having published articles, given lectures and confronted government officials with his belief in nonviolence and "respect as a human right," Massignon became an active witness in his seventies during the long and painful Algerian struggle for independence from colonial France from 1954 to 1962. This prominent scholar, linguistic genius, and former lieutenant and ambassador of France, protested in the streets of Paris out of compassion for both France and his Muslim brothers and sisters.

It was during this time that Massignon wrote his passionate prayer to Saint Joan of Arc. He spoke from his poetic imagination as if he were a marine visiting the small chapel of Our Lady of Bermont where Joan first heard the Saint's voices calling her to save France. His own life experience of two world wars and years of personal conversion as he crossed over to the other, gaining profound respect and compassion for the community of Islam and his Muslim friends, inspired his plea to Saint Joan:

> "Remember the pilgrimages to Domremy made during the war by those who continued to believe in France because of your legend, despite their loss of faith in your God? France was born again in your Virgin Heart when you were burned at the stake and your ashes were thrown into the Seine. You have marked France forever. There were those who understood your secret before you were canonized and recognized as a national heroine, that you stand for all oppressed people like your friend Mary of Nazareth did for the people of Israel, that all people may call her homeland Blessed, rather than cursing it like the ancient Biblical Nineveh and Babylon. You, who were unknown by your country like her, remember the prayers of distress that the faithful of Arab Islam address to God alone.
>
> Remember how you answered the Syrian woman who called on your name at Damascus by sweeping up the mandates for bombardment and the Moroccan Sheik who called out to you in the mosque against a regime that tortured and deported his people? He was condemned to eighteen months in prison for usurping your sacred name by the French patrons who claim ownership of it, despite appeals to the Pope.
>
> Act now in Algeria where in honor of the 500th anniversary of your rehabilitation they are preaching a crusade against a backward and undernourished people paralyzed by the violence around them, like France was in your time. One hundred years ago your sister from Kabyle, Lella Fatma of Soumeur, anticipated this obstacle when in her red coat she urged 157 Moussabbelîne from Tichkirt to chain themselves as volunteers for death to the gate of their invaded village.

Free them from the helicopters, those grasshoppers of the Apocalypse, used for surveillance in order to control your divided country.

Console the Algerian workers who came to work in France to support their families. Their families are starving in Algeria because we block their money orders and salaries at the post office. Motive: So that the Algerian partisans don't steal them. We dare to give "alms," patronizing them by giving emergency supplies to the people whose salaries we stole, sentencing France to Divine Retribution.

Finally, silence the appeals of the press in London and Paris for a "cordial agreement" based on taking advantage of Muslims and Arabs. This is not the kind of reconciliation that you would have envisioned. One like Saint Francis and Saint Louis attempted during the Crusades at Damietta which was a just resolution by the grace of the same Savior that both Islam and Christianity await.

Let me tell you the depth of my hope in you. Forty years ago I was given a joint appointment as an officer under the Arab commander, Emir Faisal, with the Englishman, Lawrence. We were to work on implementing the Anglo-French agreement to establish zones of French and British influence in the Near East which we understood as an emancipation of the Arab Orient, like the crusade of your desire. Lawrence warned me that in time we risked being "sacrificed" by the word of honor of our countries, which I only understood on the day of Meîsseloun.

You know that to love your country does not consist in making oneself a complaisant toy of those who buy and resell the host, for the host is sacred. Lawrence resigned to everything and was wounded to death by his viril loyalty, which is *le pointe vierge* in the heart of the soldier. May his living friends rise up, active penitents to the national honor of Britain.

As a Frenchman, initiated into this kind of blood fidelity by Colonialism and by the funeral of five of my fellow citizens, Algerian workers killed at the Place de la Nation the 14th of July 1953, I beg you Joan to make our country deaf to those who have betrayed her. You who have come through defeat many times, at la Chapelle Saint Denis, at Compiègne, and in prison, break through to men of compassion and nonviolence who will know how to impose the supreme mediation between two opposing terrorisms that are making a scorched land of Algeria.

In Lawrence's name, in the name of those ancients loyal in the classical manner, in the name of the hospitality that London offered many times to those French and Arabs exiled from military honor, Saint, Insurgent for Justice, Holy One, Pledged to unwritten Law, wake up noble souls who like the young Antigone were not made to live life in hatred—liberate France and England from economic enslavement—make them refind your heart."[10]

At the very end of his life Massignon once again turned to Saint Joan dedicating one of his last meditations to her in an obscure article that appeared after his death.[11] In this meditation he makes it clear that compassion does not originate with humans but is rather an "angelic visitation, a sacred wound in the heart" that allows us to offer ourselves to God for the sake of others as Joan did. She became capable of inspiring men, who lacked the kind of courage necessary to make the supreme sacrifice, like that which was demanded of Abraham. He wrote:

"....Every compassionate soul has a kind-of Open Book, invisible to others, of the examples of martyrs to imitate who she imagines to be the Breviary [Book of Prayer] common to the whole Church."[12]

In reality, he writes, these compassionate souls go towards God alone. Since his conversion Massignon had sought to live like Joan, entirely submissive to an "Order of God," offering himself in sympathy with all the sufferings on earth. This compassion, that wounded the hearts of Huysmans' long chain of substitutes, including Joan, inspired Massignon's passionate prayer to her and was what he invited the members of the Badaliya to experience with him.[13]

Chapter Seven

The Eternal Feminine
Mary and the Virgin Heart

LOUIS MASSIGNON'S father, Ferdinand Massignon was the grandson of peasants who lived in the French region called Vexin until the French Revolution in 1789. As the artist known as Pierre Roche, he had a great influence on his son, who wrote that during his childhood he woke up every morning looking at the two kakemonos trees from Japan that his father had planted in their garden. They blossomed every spring for sixty years as a reminder of how Japanese art had influenced his father's art work after he saw an exhibit of Japanese prints in Paris. Although Pierre Roche formed his style as a sculptor by carefully studying Greco-Roman and Renaissance artists, he was also attracted to the simple agricultural life of his ancestors. As we have seen, he respected Joan of Arc and her miraculous part in the history of France despite his lack of belief in God.

In 1928 Louis Massignon began a study of the beliefs of the peasants of the French Vexin, intending to write a family history for his eldest son.[1] He discovered that Joan of Arc was only one of hundreds of similar cases of devoted young peasant girls who he called "Daughters of the Parochial Vows." On May 2nd every year they became temporary priestesses of local apparitions of the Virgin Mary. They included Anne Kathryn Emmerich at Dülmen, Melanie at La Salette and Lucia at Fatima. He wrote that these apparitions were "not precisely the Jewish Virgin-Mother of conscious Christendom, but her prototype, the immemorial witnessing Virgin of Transcendence, foreseen as a common archetype from the Greek cave of Persephone in the Eleusinian Mysteries to the Japanese cave of Amaterasu-Omikami." He wrote, "After all, the only miracle humanity is longing for is The Eternal Feminine, which Goethe intuited, but here seen as a sense of inviolable virginity begetting us to life...."[2]

Massignon came to recognize this archetype of "inviolable virginity begetting us to life" as the core of Christian faith and belief, and the connecting link for all three religious traditions that identify themselves as descendants of Abraham. He is not talking about an idealized woman or a miraculous birth, but rather of an image of God, that the Islamic mystic, Hallaj called *le point vierge*, or the Virgin Heart. Hallaj writes that God can only relate to the virginal found deep in the heart of every human soul.

Massignon's writing is filled with Biblical and Koranic images. He describes God as a Stranger who visits unexpectedly like the three angels who visit Abraham in Genesis 18. Abraham's hospitality to these strangers who bring messages from God is a key to understanding Massignon's emphasis on Sacred Hospitality. When he became a Third Order Franciscan in 1931 he took the religious name, Abraham, identifying in spirit with the great patriarch of Judaism, Christianity and Islam. Massignon sees the Hebrew biblical story of Abraham's willingness to sacrifice his son Isaac out of faithfulness to God as parallel to both the Christian story of the sacrifice of Jesus, and to the desire of the Muslim Hallaj to die as a witness to God's compassion for the soul of humanity. Standing at the center of Massignon's vision of these three Abrahamic religions is Mary, the young Jewish girl whose "Yes" to God reminded Massignon of the theme of *le point vierge* found throughout the writings of Hallaj. We find Mary forever paired with Jesus in both the Gospels and the Koran. Massignon made many pilgrimages to shrines dedicated to the Virgin Mary all over the world. For him Mary's story points towards our own.

The abundance of paintings and sculptures of the Virgin Mary and the Virgin Mother and Child all over the world might mistakenly lead us to believe that we know a great deal about her. Yet Mary only appears in the Bible a few times, and those stories tell us very little. We are used to reading biographies filled with the details of a person's historical life. Instead, Mary's scant story tells us about a relationship with the Spirit of God that has inspired Christians and Muslims for generations, and leaves us feeling that we know her intimately.

Part One: The Story of Mary

A little more than 2000 years ago a young Jewish girl named Mary lived in a village called Nazareth, in Galilee, Palestine. Some ancient writings tell us that Mary's mother was called Anne and her father Joachim. The people in Nazareth were peasants who worked in the fields or at various crafts and trades. They spoke Hebrew and Aramaic and everyone was poor. Although Nazareth was part of the Roman Empire, the people were faithful to the Jewish law and traditions. In this culture girls were betrothed to be married at a very young age. Mary was only 12 or 13 but she was already engaged to a man named Joseph. We can only imagine her surprise when in a moment of solitude she had an experience of God breaking into her life which the scriptures describe as an angel appearing before her. The biblical authors called the angel Gabriel.

> "Upon arriving the angel said to her: 'Rejoice, O highly favored daughter! The Lord is with you. Blessed are you among women.' She was deeply troubled by his words and wondered what his greeting meant. The angel went on to say to her: 'Do not fear, Mary. You have found favor with God. You shall conceive and bear a son and give him the name Jesus. Great will be his dignity and he will be called Son of the most High. The Lord God will give him the throne of David his

father. He will rule over the house of Jacob forever and his reign will be without end.'

Mary said to the angel, 'How can this be since I do not know man? The angel answered her: 'The Holy Spirit will come upon you and the power of the Most High will overshadow you; hence, the holy offspring to be born will be called Son of God. Know that Elizabeth your kinswoman has conceived a son in her old age; she who was thought to be sterile is now in her sixth month, for nothing is impossible with God.' Mary said: 'I am the servant of the Lord. Let it be done to me as you say.' With that the angel left her."[3]

Mary did not understand and she was afraid. She knew that in her culture young women who became pregnant before they married their betrothed were shunned by the community and even stoned to death. She was risking her life even beyond how Joseph might react. Despite what may have fleetingly soared through her mind, Mary agreed. She said "Yes" to God.

The angel had told Mary that her kinswoman, her cousin Elizabeth, was in her sixth month of pregnancy. She knew that Elizabeth was way past childbearing age and that she had always been sterile. This was a miracle too. The angel said that nothing is impossible with God. Mary quickly set out for the town called Judah in the hill country to visit her cousin Elizabeth. Was her older cousin really six months pregnant? What would she say when she discovered that Mary too was with child?

When Elizabeth heard Mary's greeting, the scriptures tell us that her baby leapt in her womb for joy. She was so filled with the Holy Spirit that she cried out in a loud voice: "Blest are you among women and blest is the fruit of your womb. But who am I that the mother of my Lord should come to me?" Elizabeth knew right away that her cousin was with child and she also knew that Mary's child was the Lord. In fact, she gave her blessing to Mary for having trusted that the Lord's words to her would be fulfilled. Mary was grateful to Elizabeth for not only recognizing her situation but for validating her experience of God. She sang out in praise of her God in a song that we call the Magnificat:

> "My being proclaims the greatness of the Lord, my
> spirit finds joy in God my savior,
> For he has looked upon his servant in her lowliness;
> all ages to come shall call me blessed.
> God who is mighty has done great things for me,
> holy is his name;
> His mercy is from age to age
> on those who fear him.
> He has shown might with his arm;
> he has confused the proud in their inmost thoughts.
> He has deposed the mighty from their thrones
> and raised the lowly to high places.
> The hungry he has given every good thing,
> while the rich he has sent empty away.
> He has upheld Israel his servant,
> ever mindful of his mercy;
> Even as he promised our fathers,
> promised Abraham and his descendants forever."

Mary stayed with Elizabeth for three months, until her cousin gave birth. Elizabeth was not a young woman and perhaps Mary stayed to help her prepare for having a child in the house. Did they talk about the miracle that both these women were experiencing? Certainly the angel had led Mary to seek out her cousin at a time when she needed the wisdom and reassurance of an older woman. In those three months she had time to reflect on the meaning of her own pregnancy and prepare herself to face Joseph. When she returned to Nazareth Mary told Joseph that she was pregnant. He decided to release her quietly from her obligation to marry him in order to protect her from the law. Before he was able to carry out his plan, Joseph also had an experience of God breaking into his life which changed his mind. The Lord appeared before him in a dream as an angel who told him not to be afraid to take Mary as his wife because she had conceived this child by the Holy Spirit. The angel also said that they were to name their child Jesus, or *Jeshua* in Hebrew and Aramaic. Jeshua means the 'Lord is salvation' and the angel told Joseph that their child Jesus would free his people from their sins. Did he wonder what the angel meant when he said that their child would free his people from their sins?

Perhaps Joseph had heard how the Lord had spoken through the prophet Isaiah in the Hebrew scriptures of a virgin who would give birth to a son called Emmanuel, or 'God is with us.' Whether he knew the prophecy or not, he did know that he must listen to the message in his dream. He took Mary into his home as his wife. We do not know what Joseph experienced but we do know that he was touched by the divine and honored Mary's experience of God by having no relations with her.[4]

Caesar Augustus decided to continue to take a census of the known world at the time. He ordered everyone to register in the town in which they were born. Joseph and Mary, who was now at the end of her ninth month, began the journey from Nazareth, in Galilee, to a town called Bethlehem, in Judea, where Joseph was born. The road was crowded with travelers and by the time they reached Bethlehem there were no rooms left at the Inn. They were forced to find a place to stay in a cave, or a stable with a manger. Mary gave birth to her son there, and on the eighth day he was circumcised according to Jewish tradition, and given the name Jesus.

Many unusual things happened after this child was born that Mary treasured and took to heart, but they also caused her to reflect deeply on their meaning. In one account of the story, shepherds visited the newborn child because they were told by an angel of the Lord that the Messiah had been born in Bethlehem. Like every mother Mary surely thought her son was special, and then these shepherds appeared and said they heard that he was the Messiah awaited so long by all of Israel. Could it be true? According to the Jewish law, every first born son was to inherit the responsibilities and authority of his father, but he was also considered holy and belonged to God. The time came for the couple to be purified and to make an offering to the temple sanctuary in Jerusalem. This was in order to present their son to the Lord and pay the customary ransom to redeem him from service in the temple.

When Joseph and Mary came into the temple with Jesus an old woman named Anna was there deeply immersed in prayer. She was an eighty-four-year-old widow who was known as a prophetess because she spent long hours praying and fasting in the temple. Suddenly an old man named Simeon appeared. The Holy Spirit had revealed to him that he would not experience death until he had seen the Anointed one of the Lord. That very day the Spirit moved him to go to the temple. When he saw Mary and Joseph with Jesus he took the child in his arms and praised God, saying "Now, Master, you can dismiss your servant in peace. You have fulfilled your word. For my eyes have witnessed your saving deed displayed for all the peoples to see: A revealing light to the Gentiles, the glory for your people Israel." Then he blessed Mary and Joseph and turning to Mary he said, "This child is destined to be the downfall and the rise of many in Israel, a sign that will be opposed, and you yourself shall be pierced with a sword— so that the thoughts of many hearts may be laid bare." When the old woman Anna heard Simeon's words she gave praise to God and went out to speak of this child to all the Jewish people who were waiting for the deliverance of Jerusalem from the Roman Empire.[5] What did Mary think when she saw these two strangers who seemed to be waiting for her to bring her child Jesus to the temple in Jerusalem? What did the old man mean when he said that she would be pierced with a sword so that the thoughts of many hearts may be laid bare? The scripture stories don't tell us.

In another account of the story some astrologers, who knew that the Jewish people were waiting for a Messiah, or savior to liberate them from Roman rule, came to Jerusalem because they had seen an unusual star and followed it. The Roman senate had appointed a king in Judea called Herod. When he heard that the astrologers were looking for the place where the Jewish Messiah had been born he asked them to find the child and return to tell him so that he too could pay homage to the child. After the astrologers found Mary and Joseph and the child Jesus, they presented their gifts of gold, frankincense and myrrh. They returned immediately to their own country because of a dream that warned them to be wary of king Herod.

Joseph also had a dream. The Lord appeared to him and told him to take his family and flee to Egypt because King Herod was searching for the child in order to destroy him. They didn't return to Israel until after the death of king Herod. To protect themselves from Herod's son who succeeded his father as king of Judea, they returned instead to Nazareth.[6] We are not told of their life when Jesus was an infant and small child and are left assuming that during those years Mary's life was like that of every mother with small children to care for.

We only hear of them again when Jesus was twelve years old. Every year Mary and Joseph went to Jerusalem for the feast of Passover. At the end of the feast they began the long journey home assuming that Jesus was with the large group travelling together from Nazareth. After a days journey they began to look for him among their friends and relatives, but he was nowhere to be found. Mary and Joseph went back to Jerusalem and began to search for him. Have you seen our son Jesus? He's twelve years old…have you seen a boy of twelve from Nazareth? It was three days before they found him. There he was in the temple sitting in the midst of the teachers asking them questions and listening intently. His own answers caused them to be amazed at his intelligence.

Mary and Joseph were astonished to find him in the temple and Mary said to him, "Son, why have you done this to us? You see that your father and I have been searching for you in sorrow. He said to them, 'Why did you search for me? Did you not know that I had to be in my father's house?' But they did not grasp what he said to them." We are now told that Jesus went home with them and was obedient, growing in age and wisdom and grace before God and his neighbors in Nazareth. Like every mother, Mary remembered all these things from her son's infancy and childhood.[7] Despite her unusual experiences, the days and years passed with ordinary chores and family obligations. Surely Mary could not know, nor be prepared for what lay ahead.

We only have small clues to help us imagine what Mary felt when she saw her son beginning to gather a following as he talked to people in the temple and began to preach about his relationship to God. She was invited to a wedding in Cana, in Galilee, and Jesus and his disciples were also invited to the celebration. When the wine ran out Mary said to Jesus, "They have no more wine. Jesus replied, 'Woman how does this concern of yours involve me? My hour has not yet come.' His mother instructed those waiting on table, Do whatever he tells you." Then we are told that Jesus instructed the waiters to fill six stone water jars holding fifteen to twenty-five gallons each with water and take some for the head waiter to taste. Not knowing where this new wine came from the waiter was surprised at its excellent quality. He said to the groom that he had kept this choice wine until the end rather then serving it first as was the custom. This was the first sign of who Jesus really was, and we are told that it was done so that his disciples would believe in him. It seems that Mary recognized her son before anyone else, as mothers often do. From Cana she went with Jesus and his disciples to Capernaum for a few days.[8] What had it taken for Mary to accept her son's calling? How did she feel as he took more and more risks with the religious authorities and it became clear that not everyone understood him?

Once Mary came with his brothers to be with Jesus but could not get through the crowds. Someone said to him "Your mother and your brothers are standing out there and they wish to speak to you. He said to the one who had told him, Who is my mother? Who are my brothers? Then extending his hand toward his disciples he said, There are my mother and my brothers. Whoever does the will of my heavenly Father is brother and sister and mother to me."[9] Did Mary understand what her son meant? Jesus went from village to village all over Palestine preaching about God, healing some and causing many who heard him to want to follow him. There were rumors about him. Some even said he was the Messiah. And then he came to Jerusalem for the Passover feast. There was a shared meal, and a night of prayer in a garden, and then Jesus was arrested. The religious authorities brought him to the Roman governor and Mary's son was condemned to be crucified, which was the customary form of execution for common criminals.

Mary stood at the foot of the cross with her sister and Mary Magdalen and one of the disciples. "Seeing his mother there with the disciple whom he loved, Jesus said to his mother, Woman, there is your son. In turn he said to the disciple, there is your mother. From that hour onward the disciple took her into his care."[10] No mention is made of Mary when three days later the women discovered that Jesus was no longer in the tomb where they had laid him. Mary Magdalen had gone there and found the tomb empty. There was a man standing nearby who she did not recognize as Jesus until he called her by name. He appeared to others on the road to Emmaus and then met them in Jerusalem in the room where the disciples were hiding from the authorities. Before he left them he promised to send them the Holy Spirit. Mary and Jesus' brothers along with some women gathered with the disciples in the upstairs room where they were staying in Jerusalem to wait and pray. This is the last time that Mary is mentioned in the stories about the followers of Jesus.

We are left with two thousand years of images inspired by the devotions of those who have rejoiced with Mary at the birth of her son, and cried with her at the foot of the cross. We are the beloved disciples who care for her and she in turn is the mother who knows our sorrows, nurtures our wounds, and prays with us and for us.

Mary in the Koran

In every place that Mary is mentioned in the Koran, she is

always paired with Jesus. For Muslims her story is linked forever to her son. Mary's prominent place in Muslim tradition reinforced Massignon's image of her as a link between Christianity and Islam. For Muslims, the Annunciation takes place before the dawn of creation. Before the world was born there was a resounding response of "Yes" to God. We find that Mary's story in the Koran begins before her birth:

> "And when she was delivered she said: My Lord! Lo! I am delivered of a female— Allah knew best of what she was delivered—the male is not as the female; and lo! I have named her Mary, and lo! I crave Thy protection for her and for her offspring from Satan the outcast."[11]

Satan was the angel who was the first to know God. When God created Adam, human beings created in God's own image, Satan jealously guarded his place as the first to love God. He was banished from heaven for refusing to bow down to God's new creatures. We are told that from the beginning of her life Mary and her offspring were offered to Allah for protection against the pride of Satan. Allah accepted her and had her taken care of in the temple.

> "And her Lord accepted her with full acceptance and vouchsafed to her a goodly growth; and made Zachariah her guardian. Whenever Zachariah went into the sanctuary where she was, he found that she had food. He said: O Mary! Whence cometh unto thee this (food)? She answered: It is from Allah. Allah giveth without stint to whom He will."[12]

Then Mary withdrew from her people to a chamber looking East.[13] She placed a screen so as not to be seen and an angel appeared before her who looked like a man. Mary was afraid and took refuge in God as a protection, asking the man if he feared God. He told her that he was only a messenger from the

Lord sent to announce to her the gift of a holy son.

> "She said: "How shall I have a son, seeing that no man has touched me, and I am not unchaste?" "He said: So (it will be). Thy Lord saith: It is easy for Me. And (it will be) that We may make of him a revelation for mankind and a mercy from Us, and it is a thing ordained." "So she conceived him, and she retired with him to a remote place." "And the pains of childbirth drove her to the trunk of a palm-tree: She cried (in her anguish): "Ah! would that I had died before this! would that I had been a thing forgotten and out of sight!"
>
> "But (a voice) cried to her from beneath the (palm-tree): "Grieve not! for thy Lord hath provided a rivulet beneath thee." "And shake the trunk of the palm-tree toward thee, thou wilt cause ripe dates to fall upon thee."
>
> "So eat and drink and cool (thine) eye. And if thou dost see any man, say, 'I have vowed a fast to (God) Most Gracious, and this day will I enter into not talking with any human being.'"

When Mary brought her son to her kinfolk they exclaimed with surprise that she had come with an amazing thing. Because of her vow of silence she pointed to her son that he might explain the miracle to them. But they wondered how they could speak to a child still in the cradle.

> "He said: "I am indeed a servant of God: He hath given me revelation and made me a prophet;" "So peace is on me the day I was born, the day that I die, and the day that I shall be raised up to life (again)"!
>
> "Such (was) Jesus the son of Mary: (it is) a statement of truth, about which they (vainly) dispute."
>
> "And verily We gave unto Moses the Scripture and

We caused a train of messengers to follow after him, and We gave unto Jesus, son of Mary, clear proofs (of Allah's sovereignty), and We supported him with the Holy Spirit. Is it ever so, that, when there cometh unto you a messenger (from Allah) with that which ye yourselves desire not, ye grow arrogant, and some ye disbelieve and some ye slay?"[14]

"When Allah saith: O Jesus, son of Mary! Remember My favor unto thee and unto thy mother; how I strengthened thee with the Holy Spirit, so that thou spakest unto mankind in the cradle as in maturity; and how I taught thee the Scripture and Wisdom and the Torah and the Gospel; and how thou didst shape of clay as it were the likeness of a bird by My permission, and didst blow upon it and it was a bird by My permission, and thou didst heal him who was born blind and the leper by My permission; and how thou didst raise the dead by My permission; and how I restrained the Children of Israel from (harming) thee when thou camest unto them with clear proofs, and those of them who disbelieved exclaimed: This is naught else than mere magic;"[15]

"And because of their saying: We slew the Messiah, Jesus son of Mary, Allah's messenger—they slew him not nor crucified him, but it appeared so unto them; and lo! those who disagree concerning it are in doubt thereof; they have no knowledge thereof save pursuit of a conjecture; they slew him not for certain."[16]

"But Allah took him up unto Himself. Allah was ever Mighty, Wise."[17]

Part Two: The *Fiat*

Years of praying with the stories of Mary and her Son in the Gospels and the Koran inspired Massignon's images of the

Virgin Mother. From her "Yes" to God at the Annunciation, her visit to her cousin Elizabeth, the prayers of Simeon and Anna at the Presentation in the temple, to Mary's face at the foot of the Cross, Massignon helps us to find her at the core of our life in God. Such a spiritual journey can only begin when we too abandon ourselves to God, acknowledging our dependence and accepting that the "action of God's will in us"[18] will lead to life. It is the very first step. Massignon's vision of Mary was human, real and earthy, well beyond the images of her in his time. In a letter to Mary Kahil, he wrote:

> "There is no maternal grief in the world comparable to the vow, the 'fiat', of the Jewish Mary when she sacrificed the hope of her race into which the Messiah should be born, to serve God alone. Her fiat was to abandon herself totally to God in order to bring the Savior among us."[19]

By welcoming the divine Guest, Mary becomes the perfect archetype of the relationship with God to which we are all called. Over and over again in his letters to Mary Kahil and to the Badaliya Massignon wrote about Mary's "Yes" to God.

She offered herself to the Stranger and became an object of suspicion all of her life. She joined those biblical women whose apparent 'sins' were in fact avenues of God's grace in the world such as Tamar, Rahab, Esther and Ruth. Her story reminds us that God chooses ordinary people who are often poor and unnoticed to bring Grace into the world. Mary was unmarried, violating the social norms of her time, which left her unprotected by the strict laws for women, yet she listened to her spiritual intuition and obeyed the truth of her own inner voice. Massignon reminds us that conceiving and bringing her Holy offspring into the world left Mary marginalized and ultimately an outcast in her society. She continues to stand for the marginalized in our own society, men and women of color, welfare mothers, the homeless, the mentally ill and disabled, the immigrant and the refugee, the elderly, our inner city ghettos, and all who are victims of inequality and injustice; those through whom God's grace, the activity of God, unsolicited and always freely given, invites us to recognize as "angels" in our midst.[20]

In the Koran, Mary's "Yes" is also revered as a "testimony to God's Lordship in the Day of the Covenant."(Koran 7:172) The secret of the mystery of the Annunciation is the inheritance of both Muslims and Christians revealed in the virginal heart of Mary, whose "Yes" to God was offered for the salvation of all of humanity. She becomes a link to our Muslim brothers and sisters and provides an opportunity for dialogue and understanding between these two communities whose painful history continues to need reconciliation and healing.

Massignon's passionate response was to search meticulously for the sources of religious experience and the roots of compassion. There he discovers the God of Abraham who is possessive, persevering, and passionate in His love for all of us. Massignon reminds us that Abraham's God was first revealed to the Jewish people, among whom we find the young Mary. He calls her "a daughter of Abraham". He also insists that we remember the Koranic vision of the one God of Abraham as that of all three monotheistic traditions.[21]

Children of Abraham

Massignon's understanding of the three "Abrahamic" traditions and how they are forever bound to one another remains as controversial and as prophetic today as it was in his lifetime. By taking the name of Abraham when he made his vows as a Third Order Franciscan, Massignon identified himself with all three religious traditions and, like the prophets before him, he challenges us to transform our own narrow vision. Out of the depth of his prayer and reflections on the biblical stories of Abraham he finds the links that lead to Mary and her son.

He begins with the story of Abraham's debate with God in his efforts to save the city of Sodom from destruction.[22] Would God actually destroy all the innocent in the city in order to punish the guilty? Abraham finally attains God's promise not to destroy the city if Abraham can find ten righteous men there. Massignon envisions Abraham as substituting himself through his prayer for those townspeople of Sodom who would anger God by violating the two angels who were welcomed as guests in the home of Abraham's kinsman, Lot. Massignon writes:

> "But the people of Sodom did not accept even the sacrifice of Lot's own daughters....This prayer of Abraham hovers over societies doomed to perdition in order to raise up in their midst those ten righteous men in order to save them despite themselves."[23]

As children of Abraham we have to believe with Massignon that sometimes there are enough innocent people willing to offer themselves to save others from destruction. He invites us to allow God to pray from within us in order that we may save our families, towns, cities and nations, as Abraham tried to do, "despite themselves." In the biblical story, Sodom was destroyed and God's promise had yet to be fulfilled.

Next Massignon reminds us that Abraham's compassionate prayer to save Sodom led to two "cruel tests of love." Abram's wife Sarai was not able to bear any children. In those days a woman's value and self-worth was tied to her ability to give birth to sons as heirs to their father's property. Sarai requested that her Egyptian maidservant Hagar become her husband's concubine, in order that she may have sons through her. Once Hagar became pregnant, there was tension between the two women, as Sarai felt Hagar's disdain. Hagar in turn felt abused by Sarai and ran away. But a messenger of God intervened. Hagar was told to return and name her son Ishmael, which means "God has heard" in Hebrew. She was promised that her descendants would be too many to count. Abram was eighty-six when Ishmael was born.

In the ancient Hebrew tradition the sign of God's intervention in human affairs—and of the inner transformation of the human soul—is the giving of a new name. When Abram was ninety-nine years old, God made a covenant with him promising that Abram would be the father of a host of nations, and gave him the land of Canaan. He would be their God if all of Abram's descendants kept the covenant. He gave Abram the new name, Abraham, which means the "father is exalted." Sarai too was given the new name Sarah, which means "princess." When the princess was told that she was to give birth to a son at last, she laughed because she was so old. For this reason, when he was born her son was named Isaac, which means "laughed" in Hebrew. As the two boys grew and played together Sarah became jealous of Hagar's son Ishmael, fearing that her maidservant's son would share Abraham's inheritance with her own son Isaac. She demanded that Abraham send Hagar and Ishmael out into the wilderness. Once again God made a promise to Abraham, "Heed the demands of Sarah no matter what she is asking of you, for it is through Isaac that descendants shall bear your name. As for the son of the slave woman, I will make a great nation of him also, since he is your offspring."[24]

This was Abraham's first "cruel test." Two great nations were born, each declaring Abraham to be its father, and we, as Jewish and Christian, have inherited the ancient conflict between Sarah and Hagar. In those days a woman's power lay only in her son and his inheritance; so God gave each woman the son she needed to keep her dignity and self-respect. To end the argument the brothers were divided, and just as Sodom, which stands for the corruption and violence in our cities and among nations, has yet to be saved, so too the wounds of these half-brothers need to be healed. Perhaps Sarah's laughter is a prophetic voice calling Arab and Jew, Ishmael and Isaac, to play together again as they once did as children. And we, with Hagar, are called to recognize that God hears our prayers as we attempt to change a war zone into a playground in the Middle East, and every area of the world where wars are killing the children of Abraham in the name of religion.

The second "cruel test" of Abraham's faith and love for his

God was a demand that he sacrifice his son Isaac. It is hard to imagine what Sarah would have felt had she known that her husband Abraham had taken their son Isaac to Moriah intending to slaughter him as a holocaust offering to God. This test of Abraham's loyalty and trust in his God seems outrageous to us. We are relieved that God interferes at the last moment, and we know that through Isaac and his son Jacob the descendants of Abraham survive. To be called to an action that is stronger than reason—and even familial love—violates our sensibilities, but that is the definition of 'faith.'

Surely, if Sarah had known, she would have protected her son, persuaded her husband that God does not test us with such harsh commands. After all, Sarah's faith had been purified by years of barrenness and her own prayers to give birth to a son, even if it needed to be achieved through another woman. And yet, she laughed because her prayers were answered in God's own time, and she gave birth to Isaac in her old age. She would not have questioned God's promises to Abraham, and would have known in her heart what Abraham had still to come to believe, that his descendants would fill the earth like the stars in the sky. But Sarah was not aware of the danger to her son and had no voice in this drama.

The commandments of God are still too harsh for us. We cannot love our neighbor as ourselves. Even though there are men and women in our time who cannot have their own children and turn to advanced medical technologies or adoption, there are increasing numbers of abortions, incidents of child abuse and domestic violence. We have yet to be able to live side by side in loving respect and care with those who are culturally and racially different, or physically and mentally disabled. Nations of Abraham's children continue to kill each other's sons and daughters in genocides that we now call crimes against humanity. Apparently the sacrifice of Isaac was meant to be completed. A son of Abraham needed to die in order to save the world from sin and death.[25] Massignon wrote:

> "It would require the totally innocent abandon of a

Virgin Mother without human spouse to accept the obligation to offer up her son unto death."[26]

Massignon is suggesting that a young Jewish woman was chosen by God to bring into the world the child destined to complete the sacrifice of Isaac that was interrupted. His message is one the world, Jews, Christians and Muslims alike, has never been ready to hear. Mary's fiat stands at the core of the religious and secular dilemma of our time. Massignon wrote:

"From the beginning she agrees to become a betrothed woman suspected of infidelity, slandered by her neighbors, called an adulteress in the genealogical records of the city where she was born, and suspected (or ignored) for more than 2000 years by her race for which she had infinite love, because in order to save her people she laid bare the secret vow of an immaculate heart, something that was even greater than Abraham's willingness to sacrifice Isaac. For this she offered up for Israel the very root of God's justification vis-à-vis His only perfect creature in a spiritual sacrifice unimagined by the angels."[27]

The secret of the mystery of the Annunciation is our inheritance revealed in the virginal heart of Mary, whose "Yes" to God was offered for the salvation of all of humanity. She fulfilled not only the vocation of the Jewish people, but that of all of us. As with all spiritual truths, God is hidden within them. There is always a surprise, a shock to our assumptions about life and our world. God chooses unexpected and often unimaginable avenues to save us from ourselves. Hagar, Sarah, and Mary, the wives and a daughter of Abraham, were all chosen to fulfill God's promise of life.

Substitution

"To love a person is not only to desire that which God

wishes that person to be, or to glimpse that he will become it, without worrying about when or how. To love him for himself is to achieve it, not tomorrow but now, and for always, by abandoning ourselves in his place, delivering to God without reserve that which he lacks today, in order to become it. And one is able to achieve it ….in piercing through the divine tears of She, all pure, who has conceived us and engendered us holy with Him, at the Annunciation—the secret in the heart, the fiat, this royal fullness of abandonment to God—that young slave mothers discover in the first smile of their small baby; and now they sign themselves with the sign of the cross because every sign of the cross …. embraces us in the embrace of the divine Trinity by union in Mary's fiat."[28]

For Massignon, to love others into life is the mystery of Mary's *fiat*. He places her "Yes" to God in the midst of the Badaliya, for by conceiving Jesus, Mary conceives us and makes us holy with Him. Moreover every birth of a child, no matter how marginal her mother is in society, is an abandonment to God and the birth of God into the world. He ties Mary's *fiat* to her place at the foot of the Cross with the beloved disciple, painfully watching the agonizing death of her son. He understands the Badaliya as trying however poorly to express the compassion that pierces Mary's heart with the stab of the lance into the heart of her son, Jesus, which he calls an "Exchange of Heart."[29] Here is a profound understanding of Simeon's prophecy to Mary in the temple. In an outpouring of love through mystical substitution, Mary feels the sharp point of the sword as it enters the flesh of her dying son. Members of the Badaliya were answering a call to an "exchange of heart" by their vow to substitute their own lives for the sake of others.

Part Three: *Le Point Vierge,* The Virgin Heart

For Massignon, Mary was a fully human Jewish woman who

risked everything by responding with her whole heart to God in order to become a mother who loved, worried about, supported and knew her child. Yet he also experienced her as an archetype of "inviolable virginity begetting us to life," which led him to see her as an image of *le point vierge*, a theme he discovered in the context of the mystical doctrine of Hallaj that I call The Virgin Heart. The theme permeates Massignon's writing, sustaining it in a perpetual re-visioning of mystical experience as expressed by the Muslim saint. At the same time, he found the experience of the Virgin Heart lived by Mary expressed most dramatically by her willingness to abandon herself entirely to God. In the depth of the human soul God finds a dwelling place that Hallaj called *le point vierge*. Massignon envisions the human soul as feminine and God as a Stranger. Like the angel Gabriel's unexpected visit to Mary, the visitation of the Stranger shocks us like a blow that goes straight to the heart. He writes: "Before the Lord, who has struck the blow, the soul becomes a woman, she is silent, she consents..."[30]

Through years of contemplating Hallaj's mystical doctrine and the meaning of the Virgin Heart, Massignon realized how this theme is a connecting link to many others. His reflections on the Virgin Heart were incorporated into his major writings, lectures, and extensive correspondence and became an integral part of his own on-going spiritual conversion. When he "crossed over" into relationship with his Muslim friends he discovered that his own Christian religious experience was enhanced rather than threatened or diminished. He called this engagement with the Muslim community, "sacred hospitality."

Mary's acceptance of the Stranger, God's invitation to give birth to a holy child, was also an example of "sacred hospitality" in the form of her willingness to give life to God in the depths of her being. The mystery of the Virgin Heart comes alive in the story of the Visitation as well because the story is about the mystery of the spiritual life. Our souls leap, as Elizabeth's did, at the recognition of God within every human being, and know, with the wisdom of old age, that every human birth is a miracle.

Embedded in the mystery of the Virgin Heart is the Truth of two women, one very young, full of hope and trust, the other filled with the wisdom of sacred hospitality, the recognition of the divine child everywhere in everyone.[31]

Members of Sufi Orders today refer to Hallaj as a true disciple of divine love. In his travels as a mendicant preacher and spiritual master, Hallaj tried to lead his followers more deeply into his understanding of the reality of the human soul as finding its ultimate meaning in seeking unity in the divine."[32] He writes:

> "Our hearts are one single Virgin, which the dream of no dreamer can penetrate .... Which only the presence of the Lord penetrates in order to be conceived therein."[33]

The Virgin Heart refers to the secret place in the center of the human soul where God alone has access. Hallaj envisions the core of all human hearts as one, where the human and the Divine meet, unified and untouched by anything except the seed planted by God's love.

In his reflections and teachings Hallaj retains the notion of the human heart as expressed in the Koran under the heading of the "Science of Hearts." The heart is the human organ prepared by God for contemplation. It is in our hearts that our conscience is formed and there that we know and are conscious. It is in our hearts that we experience the sacred. Hallaj reaches beyond the Koran in expressing his mystical experience of the Science of Hearts. He writes:

> "The final covering of the heart, inside the nafs, which means the self, whose appetite is lustful, is the sirr, or latent personality, deep subconscious, or secret cell, walled up [and hidden] to every creature, the inviolable virgin."[34]

To Hallaj, the Virgin Heart is God's secret holy place at

the core of each of us. It is a place, a tiny point in the depth of the human soul that is completely pure, virginal, like the uncultivated, old growth forests in the Northwest, because it is where God dwells in us. That "place" remains forever whole and intact whether we are rich or poor, educated or illiterate, worthy or not, and regardless of our fear and pain, self-defeating habits or ungracious thoughts and desires.[35] It is a mystery that calls us to recognize the Transcendent in our midst and overcome our illusions of power and control. Hallaj writes:

> "God makes Himself explicit through everything that is perceived and considered; everything that one sees face to face signifies Him. And this is why I have said: I have seen nothing in which I have not seen God."[36]

The ultimate manifestation of Massignon's sacred hospitality is the divine Guest seeking hospitality in the center of every human soul. It is out of that unconscious depth that Mary answers "Yes" to God and becomes a witness to the deeper meaning of the Virgin Heart. Massignon wrote that to recognize the sacredness of life and of every human being, regardless of their differences, means to be capable of recognizing oneself in everyone,

> "in an overstretched trial of painful love, in a hypertension of self for mental identification with the other's need; when one cannot help him except by sharing, mentally, so poorly his pain. By tears, if one cannot afford blood—by the burning of his hunger, if one's breast cannot give him the milk of human kindness. Tears and blood, milk and fire are the means of the housekeeping, of the immemorial rite of hospitality and the rite of asylum."[37]

Out of the depth of his understanding of the Virgin Heart he invites us to allow a compassionate God to transform us. To set us free to negotiate, reconcile, and heal our divisions by accepting, respecting, and loving our differences, rather than fearing them and feeling threatened.

Massignon struggled for the right of asylum for Muslim refugees in France, experiencing them with compassion as friends and religious brothers because of their common heritage through Abraham and Mary. His writings have influenced the course of contemporary interreligious dialogue and his passion for God led to his increasing compassion for all human beings, the effect of deep reflection on the meaning of the Virgin Heart.

In 1959 the Trappist monk, Thomas Merton, began a correspondence with Massignon. Both men were seekers of the mystical aspects of diverse religious traditions. Merton was drawn to Massignon's increasing activism as a witness for nonviolence and was intrigued by the theme of the Virgin Heart. As a result of his own reflections and correspondence with Massignon he wrote:

> "At the center of our being is a point of nothingness which is untouched by sin and illusion, a point of pure truth, a point or spark which belongs entirely to God....this little point....is the pure glory of God in us.... It is like a pure diamond, blazing with the invisible light of heaven. It is in everybody."[38]

Massignon expands his vision of the Virgin Heart suggesting that by "providing hospitality to God in our hearts we enter the path toward mystical union and thereby risk becoming witnesses, and even outlaws, as did Hallaj." He speaks of a secret place in each human soul that we cannot betray because God alone has access to its hospitality. He calls it "the last virginal point"; our last point of honor as human beings.[39]

The images of the Virgin Heart in the writings of Massignon, Hallaj and Merton contain important contemporary messages. Believing in the Virgin Heart leads me to a conversion experience that calls for my own "Yes" to God despite my fear and lack of understanding. My conversion experience changes my relationships and opens my heart to others in true compassion and hospitality. I risk changing my habitual way of seeing the world, of making artificial distinctions between people of different nationalities, races or beliefs. And I risk waking up to my desire for communion and connection by allowing love itself to transform my vision.

I can no longer pass by homeless people as though they do not exist, nor can I make any distinction between those who have wealth, education, or position and those who do not. I can no longer deny that I too am homeless, a refugee, and a victim of social and political injustice. To believe in the mystery of the Virgin Heart is to believe in a secret place in every human soul where the sacred is given to us despite our unworthiness, failures, and human limitations. That place cannot be touched by anything I do, yet it calls me to transcend myself and see others as they are, as sacred.[40] Only then will I see the free gift of the Divine in others as "a pure diamond blazing in the light of heaven." When I fully acknowledge the truth of the Virgin Heart and contemplate the richness of its meaning, I catch a glimmer of the mystical experience of Hallaj who writes:

> "My soul is mixed and joined together with your soul and every accident that injures you injures me."[41]

For Massignon the Virgin Heart is represented for us by the archetype of "inviolable virginity begetting us to life," the Eternal Feminine soul, Mary of Nazareth, pregnant with the Spirit of God.

Chapter Eight

A Sign of Hope
*The Mystery of the Legend of the Seven Sleepers
and the Spiritual Journey*

LOUIS MASSIGNON SPENT his life searching for ways to bring Christians and Muslims together and ultimately all the children of Abraham. His lifelong search for the sources of the legend surrounding the Muslim saint al-Hallaj led him to follow the path of Islam as it spread from one culture to another. His gift for languages allowed him to dig deeply into the earliest records and oral histories found all over the Middle East and Asia. In the same way his spiritual life flourished in his passionate pursuit of the life stories of the saints, and by praying with the biblical figures found in both the Bible and the Koran. He was inspired to discover sources for the legends and devotions that survived the centuries and became part of different cultures throughout the world. He was particularly attracted to a story that is referred to in the Koran about seven Christian Saints known in the tradition as the Seven Sleepers.

Part One: The Legend of the Seven Sleepers

The story takes place in the city of Ephesus, known as Selçuk in modern day Turkey, during the reign of Emperor Decius in the year 257. At that time Christians were being persecuted.

Seven Christian soldiers named Maximilian, Mark, Matinian, Denis, John, Seraphim, and Constantin refused to obey the Emperor's command to worship the pagan gods Apollo and Athena. They fled to the mountains above the city where they hid in a cave near to the tomb of Mary Magdalene. They fell into a miraculous sleep and the entry to the cave closed up. In one version of the story a shepherd found them. Others recount how they woke up thinking that they had been asleep for one night. Since they were hungry, one of them agreed to sneak into the city to buy food. There he discovered that his coins were two hundred years old.

The year was 447 and the city was now ruled by the Eastern Roman Emperor, Theodosis II. These seven men were living witnesses of the Christian doctrine of the Resurrection of the body. The Emperor was sure that this was truly a miracle. Shortly afterwards all seven died at the same moment and the Emperor had their bodies enshrined. He ordered a church to be built at the site and absolved all the Bishops who had been persecuted for their belief in the Resurrection.

In 1928 the Austrian archeologist Franz Miltner discovered the remains of the sanctuary and the cemetery in Ephesus. There are Armenian, Coptic, Georgian, Greek, Ethiopian and Syrian versions of the story. The earliest existing text of the legend is of Syrian origin and dates from the 6th century. Both Muslims and Christians made pilgimages to the sanctuary of the Seven Sleepers in Ephesus, and the catacombs nearby indicate that many wanted to be buried there because of the association of the legend to the doctrine of the Resurrection. The pilgrimages were discouraged with the rise of Turkish influence.[1]

The Story in the Koran:

The legend of the seven martyrs of Ephesus from the first centuries of Christianity is referred to in the Koran in Sura XVIII. The Koran suggests that there was a dog with the Christian martyrs and brings into question how many Christians there were. It is God (Allah) who seals up the cave to protect them. The Koran also suggests that they woke up

300 plus nine years after they fell asleep. Massignon was first introduced to the story in the version of it found here:

> "Or deemest thou that the People of the Cave and the Inscription are a wonder among Our portents? When the young men fled for refuge to the Cave and said: Our Lord! Give us mercy from Thy presence, and shape for us right conduct inour plight.
> Then We sealed up their hearing in the Cave for a number of years. And afterward We raised them up that We might know which ofthe two parties would best calculate the time that they had tarried.
> We narrate unto thee their story with truth. Lo! they were young men who believed in their Lord, and We increased them in guidance. And We made firm their hearts when they stood forth and said: Our Lord is the Lord of the heavens and the earth. We cry unto no God beside Him, for then should we utter an enormity. These, our people, have chosen (other) gods beside Him though they bring no clear warrant (vouchsafed) to them.
> And who doth greater wrong than he who inventeth a lie concerning Allah? And when ye withdraw from them and that which they worship except Allah, then seek refuge in the Cave; your Lord will spread for you of His mercy and will prepare for you a pillow in your plight. And thou mightest have seen the sun when it rose move away from their cave to the right, and when it set go past them on the left, and they were in the cleft thereof. That was (one) of the portents of Allah. He whom Allah guideth, he indeed is led aright, and he whom He sendeth astray, for him thou wilt not find a guiding friend.
> And thou wouldst have deemed them waking though they were asleep, and We caused them to turn over to the right and the left, and their dog stretching out his paws on the threshold. If thou hadst observed them

closely thou hadst assuredly turned away from them in flight, and hadst been filled with awe of them.

And in like manner We awakened them that they might question one another. A speaker from among them said: How long have ye tarried? They said: We have tarried a day or some part of a day, (Others) said: Your Lord best knoweth what ye have tarried. Now send one of you with this silver coin unto the city, and let him see what food is purest there and bring you a supply thereof. Let him be courteous and let no man know of you.

For they, if they should come to know of you, will stone you or turn you back to their religion; then ye will never prosper. And in like manner We disclosed them (to the people of the city) that they might know that the promise of Allah is true, and that, as for the Hour, there is no doubt concerning it.

When (the people of the city) disputed of their case among themselves, they said: Build over them a building; their Lord knoweth best concerning them. Those who won their point said: We verily shall build a place of worship over them. (Some) will say: They were three, their dog the fourth, and (some) say: Five, their dog the sixth, guessing at random; and (some) say: Seven, and their dog the eighth. Say (O Muhammad): My Lord is Best Aware of their number. None knoweth them save a few. So contend not concerning them except with an outward contending, and ask not any of them to pronounce concerning them. And say not of anything: Lo! I shall do that tomorrow, Except if Allah will. And remember thy Lord when thou forgettest, and say: It may be that my Lord guideth me unto a nearer way of truth than this. And (it is said) they tarried in their Cave three hundred years and add nine.

Say: Allah is Best Aware how long they tarried. His is the Invisible of the heavens and the earth. How clear of sight is He and keen of hearing! They have no protecting friend beside Him, and He maketh none to share in His government."[2]

Journey to Ephesus

Twenty years before he actually visited Ephesus Massignon was already giving lectures about the cave of the Seven Sleepers. Here was a legend that clearly belonged to both Muslims and Christians and had continued to inspire devotion for centuries. When he finally began his search for the origins of the legend of the Seven Sleepers in 1951, he visited the archeological excavation of the sanctuary and cemetery in ancient Ephesus associated with the legend. Although her remains were moved, first to Constantinople and later to Saint-Baume in France, there is a church in a grotto near the cave of the Seven Sleepers dedicated to the original burial place of Mary Magdalene, who was the first to witness the Resurrection of Jesus. There is also a church called The House of the Virgin Mary nearby and a basilica with the tomb of the Apostle John. In Christian tradition Mary lived in Ephesus under the care of the disciple John until her death, called *Dormition* or "falling asleep" in the Eastern tradition, when her body and soul were believed to be taken intact into heaven. Massignon was struck by the proximity of these three sacred sites in ancient Ephesus all witnessing to the earliest Christian belief in the Resurrection. Long ago both Muslim and Christian pilgrims travelled here out of devotion to these saints and martyrs found in both traditions.

Massignon writes that it is difficult to anticipate which archetypal or even folkloric themes will catch the popular imagination and give life to sacred texts. We have to study artistic monuments that capture meditations on sacred themes; paintings, miniatures, the symbolism associated with numbers, calligraphies, icons and above all the liturgical prayers of the faithful devoted to heroic historical personalities. He was looking for the way the Gospel and ancient devotions and legends were absorbed into the liturgies because of popular intuition, and therefore informed the development of the feasts adopted by the Church. It is in the prayer life, devotions and spirituality of the faithful in all traditions that the sacred finds expression, and beliefs and dogma take shape.[3]

Massignon asks why there are sanctuaries dedicated to the Seven Sleepers in so many Muslim countries when Islamic Law forbids any artistic representation of the Divine or the saints. He suggests that sanctuaries were allowed because this is the only reference in the Koran to the Muslim belief in the divine promise of the Resurrection by Justice at the end of time. The Koran says that the people will build a place of worship over the seven saints which encouraged the popular devotion and construction of sacred places in honor of them.

Massignon connects the stories from the Bible, and the sanctuaries built at their historical sites in Jerusalem, to the spiritual meaning of the story of the Seven Sleepers. In the Gospels when Lazarus dies he is laid in a tomb which is described as a cave with a stone laid across it. He is there for three days before Jesus comes. When Jesus sees Lazarus' sisters Mary and Martha weeping with sorrow he calls Lazarus out in a loud voice to demonstrate the glory of God to them. For Christians this story also points to the general Resurrection at the end of time which is depicted by the Church of the Holy Sepulchre in Jerusalem. It was built over the site where Jesus was buried for three days in a tomb, or cave, with a large stone closing the entrance, and from which Jesus was Resurrected. For Israel, the Resurrection of Justice at the end of time is found in the vision of the prophet Ezekiel as he walked on the plain covered with dry bones and God promised to raise the whole house of Israel from their graves. These examples from Christianity and Judaism are what the cave of Ephesus has been about for thirteen centuries in Islam, whose living faith in the Resurrection at the end of time is based on these seven Christian martyrs who were buried alive in a cave.[4] What is remarkable is that almost everywhere the Seven Sleepers were forgotten in Christianity.

Part Two: The Mystery of the Seven Sleepers in Brittany

All of his life Massignon spent every summer in the province of Brittany. In this part of France, Celtic folklore is alive. Every village honors their local saints with ancient chapels and churches whether or not they are recognized officially by Rome. This ancient land remains alive with the mystery of the huge standing stones known as "menhirs" that date from 5000 to 3000 BC. The engineering skill that left a trail of huge stones all the way to Scandinavia rivals the great Egyptian Pyramids. The most recent theory of who built them and why suggests a late Neolithic and early Bronze Age seafaring race marking their path. But folklore and ancient rituals that have come down to us in the form of local customs seem to suggest more profound meanings and supernatural powers. The computer has allowed the most current theory that the stones were designed as observatories for an ancient form of astronomy.

The oldest of these ancient megaliths is the Dolmen. In Breton *dol* means flat and *men* means stone. Dolmens were designed to form large flat boxes, with one side open, to serve as burial chambers which were then covered with great mounds of earth. Driving along the roads of Brittany there are signs indicating that an ancient megalith is nearby, either a group, or an individual tall standing stone, or a Dolmen. Sometimes an uncovered Dolmen can be found at the end of a dirt road standing in an obscure corner of someone's private farm. Because of the folkloric and "pagan" rituals associated with the megaliths the Church tended to "Christianize" them by associating them with stories of the saints and even sculpting them into statues in honor of the saint to whom the church was dedicated. It is not unusual in Brittany to drive by a church with one or more menhirs standing boldly in the churchyard with a cross or the figures of saints sculpted into the top.

There is always the sense in the Celtic world that well before the advent of Christianity the people felt their intimate connection with the divine. Long before the Celtic invasions of Brittany in the 5th century Bretons celebrated the religious rituals and festivals of the ancient Druids. Today the tradition continues in the form of pilgrimages, or retreats, called *pardons*, which take place all over Brittany from March to October. These colorful pilgrimages call the faithful to ask forgiveness for their sins, to pray for healing and even miraculous cures, but they also include blessings of local occupations like fishing, and the harvest of grains, fruit, or oysters. They often take place in tiny ancient chapels built more than a thousand years ago and are dedicated to local saints who are revered by the people for their holiness and dedication to local needs.

Every *pardon* includes a celebration of Mass for a pardoning of sins, a procession carrying statues of the saints or relics, and the singing of hymns, sometimes in ancient Breton. The procession led by the local Bishop or Priest often leads the long trail of villagers dressed in their local traditional costumes to the site of their daily work, to the sea or oyster bed, for a blessing. The rest of the day is a great feast of local dishes, traditional folk dancing, music, and celebration. Every *pardon* has its roots in an ancient legend which is often read aloud during the celebration.

Massignon not only found Islamic places dedicated to the Seven Sleepers in Algeria, Egypt, Turkey and Morocco but also Christian sites in the Middle East. He was more surprised to find churches in Spain and Germany and he did not expect to find one in France, particularly not one so close to his home in Brittany. He was looking for signs from the earliest centuries of Christianity of the path of evangelization in France. The maritime ports of call on the trade route between Ireland and the Middle East provided a clue as to how the Eastern church and its devotions found their way to Brittany with the Celtic immigration in the 5th century. He found churches devoted to the Eastern *Dormition*, or "falling asleep," of the Virgin Mary along the river in the region of Lannion in Brittany. In Lannion, in the tiny hamlet of Stiffel in the village of Vieux Marché near Plouaret, Massignon found a chapel called *La Chapelle des Sept Dormants*, The Chapel of the Seven Sleepers.

In the process of doing research on popular devotions in

Brittany Massignon's daughter, Geneviève told her father about some curious inconsistencies about the origins of this chapel. In 1953 Massignon attended the *pardon* which traditionally took place on the Sunday following July 22, the feast day of Mary Magdalen in the Roman Church calendar. He was intrigued by the reading, chanted in ancient Breton, of the original legend associated with the *pardon*. There were other things about this chapel that also caught his attention.

On the corner stone of the chapel there is still an inscription of the original dedication dated July 22, 1703, the feast of Mary Magdalen. The chapel was built between 1703 and 1714. In the crypt of the church there is a dolmen and nearby there is a natural spring which is called "Stiffel" in Breton, literally a "fountain from which natural spring water flows from a rock." This was strikingly similar to Muslim sites dedicated to the Seven Saints established near to a natural spring, such as the one in Sétif, Algeria, and near to sanctuaries dedicated to both Mary Magdalen and the Virgin Mary, as in Ephesus. In the sanctuary in Vieux Marché seven ancient statues of the Seven Sleepers line the altar with the Virgin Mary centered between them.

Although the villagers had assumed for years that the chapel and its *pardon* were associated with seven Bishops from the early church in the area, the similarities and correspondences with the sanctuaries in the Middle East dedicated to the Seven Saints of Ephesus aroused Massignon's curiosity. His research began with a translation of the Breton legend called a *gwerz*. He discovered that it was strikingly different from the traditional Breton legends, which usually focused on the history of the chapel, lives of the saints and the rebuilding of the chapels after the wars that destroyed them. Here was an account that celebrated the crypt with its dolmen; the spring, called a *Source* in French, with water streaming from seven veins in the rock; and the story of the Seven Saints of Ephesus. It seemed to come from an ancient tradition well before the chapel was built in the early eighteenth century. Here are some of the lines that resemble the story of the Seven Sleepers in the Koran.

The *Gwerz*

After inviting the participants to listen carefully to this spiritual canticle because it will bring joy to their hearts the next stanza asks them to turn their hearts and their prayers towards heaven. It states:

> "I assure you that you will then see something absolutely certain, and I am speaking to you of a work that was not made by human hands.
>
> In the diocese of Tréguier, in the parish of Plouaret/ The Holy Spirit erected a Chapel/ without limestone, without clay, nor mason, nor roofer, nor carpenter/ those who come to see it, will see that this is true.
>
> The Chapel was only made with six stones/four serving as walls/ and two others for the roof: who would not understand/ That only God Almighty was able to build it?
>
> You will ask perhaps/ when and how it was built; /and I respond: that I believe that when the world was created, / the sky, the sea, the earth, it was also built."

The next stanzas tell the pilgrims that the Seven Saints, who prayed in this Chapel, served God when they were on earth and now that they are in their glory are defending them. The Mother of Mercy, Mary, is also there in the middle of the Saints helping the pilgrims to be forgiven by her Son when they come to ask the "Seven Brothers" to pray for them. The Seven Saints are named in the Western tradition of the story. Then the legend is told of the cruel Emperor Decius who persecuted Christians making martyrs of those who refused to abandon their faith. The seven brothers of Ephesus vowed to be seven martyrs rather than to disavow the crucified Christ.

In this Breton version of the story when the seven hid in a cave they were discovered and masons were ordered to cruelly seal up the entrance, burying them alive. There they remained for 177 years.

"When the Seven Saints were buried in the cave / by the power of God they began to sleep/ seventeen and eight times twenty years (177) they were, without awakening/ and when the cavern was opened, they found them there."

The news of the miracle spread everywhere and all the people of Ephesus came to see them.

"By the testimony of a metal plaque, found there next to them/ where their names and their lives were written/ God permitted, for His great glory/ knowledge of how much time they had been enclosed.

Soon after, Death arrived to the Seven Saints / their souls brought to heaven in one stroke".

What a great treasure the Bretons have in the parish of Plouaret.

"Besides the pretty little chapel, there is also, near to it/ a beautiful Fountain of the Seven Saints, and it has seven veins/ seven streams by which God gives graces/ and for all time He continues to do many miracles."[5]

It appeared to Massignon that here in Brittany, transported far from its origins, this ancient Eastern devotion to the Seven Sleepers took on universal significance. The traditional *pardon* provided an opportunity to bring Christians and Muslims together spiritually through this miraculous story found in both traditions. Here in this place made sacred by the rituals of ancient peoples even before the advent of Christianity, an ancient devotion had made it's way to Celtic Brittany, connecting East and West. A chapel, dedicated to the Seven Sleepers and the hope of Resurrection, built over a dolmen near to a grotto with a natural spring with seven veins, was surely sacred ground. Massignon envisioned expanding the local *pardon* at Vieux Marché into an annual pilgrimage for both Christians and Muslims.

On July 24, 1954, as an offering dedicated to the protection of Abraham, the father of all monotheistic believers, Massignon introduced the first shared Christian/Muslim pilgrimage at Vieux Marché. Every year, until his death in 1962, Massignon participated in a procession of light, called "the fire of joy" in the cloisters. Seven symbolic candles were lit. Then, gathering the pilgrims together at the fountain of the seven veins of the Stiffel, he read the verses from the Koran related to the Seven Sleepers in Arabic, followed by a translation in French. The Bishop gave permission for a Greek Catholic Mass in Arabic early in the morning before the *pardon*. Christians from the Middle East and well known Muslim scholars came together with North African laborers from the outskirts of Paris, who had taken the literacy courses that Massignon had voluntarily organized and taught from 1929 until his death. He was able to gain official recognition of the chapel as a Historic Monument.

Part Three: The Spiritual Journey

The Chapel

Following the road signs pointing towards the center of the village of Vieux Marché brings us to the local Church and square that marks the center around which every Breton town is traditionally built. The narrow village streets lined with shops branch out from the square and become what appears to be solid walls on both sides of the street. Only a doorway or shuttered window along the way suggests the homes and courtyards hidden behind them. A small sign in the shape of an arrow on one corner of a street leading into the square points the way to our chapel saying simply, "Les Sept Dormants," The Seven Sleepers. The road winds its way out of the village and is soon lined with the beautiful cultivated fields typical of Brittany's countryside. It feels like a long drive and we wonder if we are going the right way when we find ourselves passing through a lane of plane trees, their branches hanging over the road from both sides like a covered entrance way. The road turns to the right with an open field on one side and a few buildings on the other. Before us on the left stands an ancient chapel. There is a blue plaque hanging on the gate which describes the chapel of the Seven Saints who have been venerated here for several centuries. It identifies them as the Seven Sleepers of Ephesus with a brief description of their story. The last paragraph reads:

> "These martyrs to the faith are revered by Christians and Moslems alike. The 18th Sura of the Koran, 'Ahl al-Kahf" (The Cave) read every Friday in the mosques tells their story. Their cult reached here, brought by traders from the east who followed the tin route. Inspired by Louis Massignon, oriental professor at the Collège de France, an Islamic-Christian pilgrimage has been combined with the traditional pardon every year since 1954 on the fourth Sunday in July."

On the door at the main entrance to the chapel a hand written paper sign in French invites those visitors who wish to enter the chapel to ask for the key at the convenience store. One of two buildings not far away turns out to be the right place and we are given a large old fashioned key to the side entrance. Entering we turn to face the sanctuary. There on a stone altar the Seven Saints stand carved of wood with the Virgin centered between them. The chapel is shaped in the form of a cross with the two side altars displaying statues of various saints and angels high above us. It is a climb up the long granite steps, each three feet high, to reach them. From there we are closer to the large statue of the crucified Jesus mounted on wooden cross beams hanging over the center of the chapel.

Below the building in the crypt, the dolmen is walled in on all sides and covered by the floor of the main chapel. At the end, on a primitive stone altar, are the original ancient statuettes of the Seven Sleepers carved in wood or stone which were the models for the statues later placed in the main chapel. It is this crypt that the Breton *gwerz* claims was not made by human hands and built by God when the world was created.

For Louis Massignon and those who come as pilgrims every year this Breton chapel contains far more than a legend. In his opening prayer in 1954 to begin the first gathering of Christian and Muslim pilgrims coming together for the annual *pardon*, Massignon invites them to remember their roots in the Hebrew tradition, pointing out that this was the feast day of the prophet Ezekiel in the Eastern Christian churches.

> "[Ezekiel] is the one who God made see a great plain filled with dry bones. They were his people, the people of Israel. And God said to him: Do you think that these dry bones will ever come back to life? Cry out to them: "dry bones, listen to the Word of God." And they will rise up.
>
> The pilgrim to whom he gave the word this evening, has visited the holy place on the banks of the Euphrates twice where the prophet Ezekiel shouted the word of resurrection. And if he remembers it this evening before this dolmen which has become a Christian crypt, it is because the apostles, witnesses of the resurrection of Christ, coming from the East to Brittany consecrated this tomb of dead pagans, their dry bones, to the Seven Martyrs of Ephesus…these seven Martyrs were buried alive by a tyrant, and were revived many years later, for a brief moment, witnesses, anticipating like Lazarus, our future Resurrection by Justice.
>
> The dedication of this dolmen is a proof, a monolithic promise to us as well, of our Resurrection by Justice."[6]

In his carefully documented research on the origins of this chapel in Brittany, Massignon was convinced that the Christianization of the crypt with the dolmen of Stiffel occurred in the sixth century rather than in the chapel's eighteenth century dedication. For Massignon the key to his conviction lay in the second to fifth stanzas of the *gwerz*. He wrote:

> "[these stanzas state] the certitude that the cult in this place was primitive; this dolmen was not a temple that was made by human hands but it is the Holy Spirit that had it erected to the true God.... The pagans who would have had the inspiration to erect it raised it up to the living God, to the One to whom the Seven Sleepers buried in their cave, and all dead believers buried in their tombs, render silent testimony, century after century, awaiting the resurrection."[7]

Massignon invites us to extend our spiritual connections, even back to primitive pre-biblical people, and see in them the work of the Holy Spirit. Our spiritual lives are mysteriously bound to the signs of God's action in our lives hidden in ancient dolmens and crypts awaiting our hope of resurrection into the fullness of life. Explaining his feelings about this *pardon* he wrote:

> "It is furthermore the intuition, after having visited the crypt in Ephesus, of a genealogical and topographical solidarity that I have experienced in the context of meditating on the theme of the Resurrection of the dead in the megalithic era, by coming to pray with the Breton parishioners with whom I have already made the traditional procession and fire of joy three times in the pilgrimage to the Seven Saints."[8]

The Cave

There are many versions of the legend of the Seven Sleepers in Islam and the symbol of the cave is rich with spiritual meaning. In some Muslim traditions the seven saints have come to represent the realization of the highest ideal of Islamic mysticism. In the Koran the only valid monastic rule is that one depends on God alone. Refusing to betray their beliefs these seven saints put themselves entirely in the hands of their God and hid from their persecutors in a cave. And it was God who protected them. In the first centuries of Christianity those known as the Desert Fathers lived in caves where they prayed in solitude leaving us a legacy of early Christian spiritual writings. In the 12th century Saint Francis also retreated to a cave for solitary prayer. Massignon quotes a commentary that became an authoritative statement for both Turkish Sunnite mystics and Persian Shi'ites. It was written at the time of the official rehabilitation of al-Hallaj and reminds us of the prophets speaking on behalf of their God. It says: "In God's community there are mystics whose state of being is more astonishing than that of the Seven Sleepers. They choose to retreat from the world and seek asylum in a "cave" which is a House of Recollection, the mark of love inscribed in their hearts."

> "If the People of the Cave sought asylum in a Cavern for fear of the encounter with Decius, these have taken asylum in the Cave of Retreat through the desire to encounter Me. And if their desire in saying, 'Give us our share' was to ask to be saved from Decius and to come out of the Cavern healthy and safe, the desire of these others is to be saved from their own inner malice and to come out of the shadows of this existence in order to arrive at the clarity of My splendor and My glory."[9]

On January 7, 1955 Massignon wrote to Mary Kahil that it was through Hallaj that he came to know the Seven Sleepers. They were like Mary who after the Annunciation "pondered all these things in her heart" before they came to life outside of her. The fact that Hallaj died in the year dedicated to the Seven Sleepers symbolized the consummation of love in a heart subject solely to the direction of God. Massignon found it remarkable that this Christian story reappeared in Islam. He wrote:

"…..this resurrection anticipated by the Seven Sleepers who did not wait for the Judge to call them with the others; their amorous impatience released them in order to testify for a short instant. The bursting out of these seven buds before the eternal Spring, the hard opening which makes cutting the rose with seven petals snap before the night dew, is Jesus who, in the depth of their hearts, made the seals of the cave where they were buried fly off. Let us call him like them so that He shatters our prison."[10]

Massignon saw the importance in both Islam and Christianity of the spiritual connection of the cave of the Seven Saints with the Virgin Mary and Mary Magdalene. Externally there is the physical presence of the church, called The House of the Virgin Mary, near to the first cavern in Ephesus, as well as a church in a grotto nearby dedicated to the original burial place of Mary Magdalene. The inner spiritual journey is like entering the "cave" of one's own heart in order to find God. Just as Jesus is conceived by the Holy Spirit and nurtured in the "cave-like" womb of Mary in order to give birth to God in the world, the "cave" of the human heart contains the Virgin Heart, *le pointe vierge*, the unaccessible dwelling place of God in the center of the soul of every human being.

The tomb of Mary Magdalene in Ephesus at the edge of the Cave of the Seven Sleepers, alongside the basilica of Saint John contains a mystery that Massignon continued to explore in his reflections throughout his life. Here was the first witness to the Resurrection, Mary Magdalene, mysteriously guarding the fasting and perpetual silence of these first monastic hermits who were buried alive and momentarily resurrected. Here too was a monument to Saint John, the disciple who Massignon calls the first "substitute" designated by Christ from the Cross when he places his mother, Mary, under John's protection saying, "Woman, there is your son." And turning to the disciple saying, "There is your mother. And from then on the disciple took her into his care."

Here is a mysterious trilogy where Mary finds herself with the disciple John, Mary Magdalene and the Seven Sleepers in Ephesus connecting her Dormition, or falling asleep, forever to the Resurrection. For Massignon the whole story of our hope in the mystery of the Resurrection is here in Ephesus, transported to the *pardon* celebrated by Muslims and Christians to this day at the Chapel of the Seven Sleepers in Brittany.

On July 21, 1945, the Feast of Mary Magdalene in the Roman Church, Massignon shared this prayer in a letter to Mary Kahil:

> "[Mary Magdalene was] ...the first who cried out our joy in Your Resurrection! You had forgiven her, but she had need of this Triumph of Love in order to be transfigured by Your purity, set like a seal on Your Heart, placed like a seal on Your arm: and Your Resurrection is necessary for us also in order that Your love for us, and outside of us, triumph..."[11]

For Massignon the fact that the cult of the Seven Sleepers found itself re-rooted in various cultures around the world was a testimony to the mystery of its spiritual meaning. The tomb of Mary Magdalene near the cave in Ephesus is a powerful reminder of the spiritual meaning of her story for us. He reminds us that she was the sister of Lazarus who she loved. He, like the seven brothers, was temporarily brought back to life by her Lord. Early Easter morning it was she who went to anoint Jesus' body thinking that he too had died. But the tomb was empty, and for a brief moment he appeared to her. And now she is buried on the threshold of the cave of Ephesus waiting with us for him to come back.[12] It was not by accident that the Chapel of the Seven Sleepers in Vieux Marché was dedicated on her feast day, July, 22, 1703.

On June 29, 1962 just four months before his death, Massignon wrote to Mary Kahil:

> "One word on the Seven Sleepers and on our offering

and common faith, at least on one point, as tenuous as it is, the resurrection. What else is there to hope for with the 'buried alive' than the Resurrection prefigured by the reappearance of these seven Lazarus' from the cave of Ephesus, on the threshold of which was the burial place, in the faith in the Resurrection with Christ and through Christ, of the sister of Lazarus, the Magdalene? Such is the principal testimony of Ephesus."[13]

The Source

In Celtic tradition ancient megaliths were often built next to natural springs where water spills out through the rocks from sources deep within the earth. The natural spring was sacred and became a place of healing, ritual, and burial rich with symbolic meaning as well as a practical source of minerals and life-giving pure drinking water. The Stiffel in Breton not only means a fountain with its source from a rock but also indicates the use of the water for a laundry, outwardly a place for cleansing clothing and spiritually a place for cleansing the human soul. In his careful translation of the *gwerz* Massignon points to the importance of the fountain with its seven veins near to the ancient sacred dolmen and crypt of the chapel of the Seven Sleepers. These are healing waters and a place chosen by God to represent a mysterious archetype that continues to give life everywhere that the story of the Seven Saints appears in the culture. The ancient Breton *gwerz* states:

> "This fresh water, was fortified with energy, and cured a few/ calmed the pain of some who were sick/ God gave to souls fine graces/ and to bodies energy and health/ through the intercession obtained by the Seven Saints.
>
> There is not a place on earth, when we come there to pray/ where God is unable to accept our offering/ It is true just the same, that He has chosen places, above all

other places, to be honored there.

A chapel with seven stones, raised for a very long time/ a Fountain with seven sources, where many miracles have happened/ makes us clearly see that the Seven Saints are a place/ that God has chosen in order to give us graces."[14]

Reconciliation: The Children of Abraham

To the very end of his life Massignon fervently believed in the mission of the Badaliya and the shared experience of Christians and Muslims praying on pilgrimage together at the Chapel of the Seven Sleepers in Brittany. He wrote many letters to friends encouraging them to work towards the survival of the Badaliya and the pilgrimage. In his spiritual life he had come to fully embrace the desire to abandon himself to God that he had experienced on his first terrifying encounter with the Divine in Baghdad in 1908. For Massignon the stories from all three religious traditions of the Seven Sleepers, Hallaj, Abraham and the Virgin Mary are examples of how we are all called to abandon ourselves to God.

In praying for the survival of the Badaliya and the pilgrimage to the Seven Sleepers in Brittany he was expressing the key to his spiritual orientation that experienced hospitality as the highest form of love. By accepting, respecting, and ultimately loving others we are welcoming the God that Massignon called the "Stranger," into our hearts. He spent his life praying for Muslims and finally taking social action on behalf of all religious division and persecution. This letter suggests what his identification with Abraham meant to him. He wrote:

"I care a lot about going to Hebron: it is the tomb of Abraham, the Patriarch of Believers, Jews, Christians and Muslims. He is also the first hero of hospitality, of the right to asylum, and respect for the stranger."[15]

In his annual letter to members of the Badaliya Massignon wrote out of his profound belief in the efficacy of prayer:

> "Our work, more than ever, is to understand from the inside, the recovery of the collective conscious which binds the world's Muslim believers together more and more, through thinking of them as brothers, in order to prepare for the reconciliation between all the children of Abraham.
>
> It is necessary, and this is more difficult, to not limit our compassionate substitution only to oppressed Muslims to whom the Badaliya is consecrated. ....To defend the oppressed without working to touch the hearts of the powerful sometimes succeeds, alas, in sustaining a vengeful class struggle turning back against the powerful to become in their turn the oppressed.
>
> It is necessary to bear witness, to claim truth and justice peacefully with serene nonviolence. ...Thus we must transform, little by little, good conscience to good thoughts by authentic Christian compassion, waiting before reproaching them, until they are in a state to understand. We wanted to move quickly, it is difficult not to be able to immediately rescue harsh suffering other than through silent prayer, fasting, and sacrificing oneself. But yet, this is the example of the Lord throughout his Passion. We ask Him to bring us there with him in forgiving those among us who have not yet understood;..."[16]

Once a month Massignon encouraged members of the Badaliya to fast for peace between Christians and Muslims and finally all the children of Abraham. Many joined him from all three traditions. In 1953 Massignon chose September 19th for the fast for peace. In Christianity it is the feast of the appearance of Our Lady of La Salette at whose shrine J.-K. Huysmans prayed for his conversion. It was on September 19, 1951 that

Massignon first visited Ephesus. The famous Jewish philosopher Martin Buber joined them in their fast. Massignon wrote to him:

> "...thus we will fast under the same conditions as previously, from the rising to the setting of the sun September 19, for the reconciliation in justice of our three communities coming from Abraham: Israel, Christianity and Islam."[17]

For a gathering of the Badaliya on June 1, 1962, five months before his death, Louis Massignon wrote these words which we still need to hear:

> "....Let us not grow weary of repeating that it is necessary to pray together as Christians and Jews and Muslims, for the advent of this so desired Peace, for which we have waited so long. Every tentative agreement on economic grounds and even cultural, if it is not founded on a sincere movement of hearts, united in Faith in the God of Abraham, Father of all Believers, will only scare the third world and throw it back to the camp of professional atheists."[18]

The pilgrimage in Vieux Marché, shared by Christians and Muslims and many Jewish friends who prayed with them in spirit, became a symbol of Massignon's own spiritual journey towards reconciliation and the One God who heals all divisions. He left us the words of Hallaj who said with the seven Christian martyrs, "God, and that is everything."[19]

A Sign of Hope

Afterword

After Massignon's death in 1962 an Institute was established in Paris called the Friends of Louis Massignon which continues to sponsor and attend the annual *pardon*. To this day the prayers and readings from the Koran at the ancient Source near the chapel in Vieux Marché begin the celebration of the *pardon* every year.

In July 2000, Louis Massignon's son, Daniel, and his family attended the celebration along with Christian and Muslim guests, the local population, and members of the Association of which he had been the President since 1965. In 1992 the Massignon Institute was legally established to promote further research and translation of Louis Massignon's scholarly writings and spiritual legacy. On December 25, 2000, Daniel Massignon died in his home in Paris. Every year from July 1963 to July 2000 he substituted for his father at the pilgrimage by reading the story of the Seven Sleepers aloud to the community.

Daniel and Nicole Massignon encouraged and supported me throughout the writing of this book. I am ever grateful for Daniel Massignon's personal contributions, the last of which arrived at the end of November 2000.

Notes

Introduction

1. Destremau/Moncelon 1994. Massignon Paris, PLON, p. 57

Chapter One

1. Baldick, R. 1955. The Life of J.-K.Huysmans. Oxford: Clarendon Press. p. 354

2. ibid., p. 6-7

3. ibid., p. 67

4. ibid., p. 69

5. ibid. 87

6. ibid., p.143

7. ibid., p.147 from an essay, Les Sataniques of Félicien Rops

8. ibid., p. 206

9. ibid., p. 182

10. ibid., p. 194. Narfon (Julien de) 'Le Cahier de l'Abbé Mugnier' in Le Figaro, October 5, 1907

11. ibid., p. 197

12. ibid., p. 201

13. ibid., p. 216

14. ibid., p. 247 letter to the artist Forain, January 1901

15. ibid., p. 266

16. ibid., p. 290 quoted in Bontoux (Henri) pp. 220-224 Les Étapes de Dehival dans les voies de l'amour, Beauchesne, 4th ed. 1926

17. ibid., p. 276

18. Destremau, C. and Moncelon, J. 1994. Louis Massignon. Paris: PLON, p. 23

19. Baldick, R. p. 290

20. Huysmans, J.-K. 1923. trans. Hastings, A. Saint Lydwine of Schiedam. Rockford, IL.: Tan Books and Publishers, Inc. p. 42

21. ibid., p. 63

22. ibid., p. 68

23. Baldick p. 315

24. ibid., p. 347

25. ibid., p. 351 Retté (Adolphe) 1914. In Quand l'Esprit Souffle, Messein, 2nd ed.

26. ibid., p. 351 Bernaërt (Édouard). pp. 16-17 'Huysmans Intime' in L'Univers, November 1908

27. Lydwine p. 28

28. ibid., p. 221

29. Luke 22:44

30. Baldick p. 314

31. Lydwine p. 158

32. ibid., p. 154

33. ibid., p. 157

34. ibid., p. 158

35. Gude, M.L. 1996. Louis Massignon: The Crucible of Compassion. Notre Dame, IN and London: University of Notre Dame Press. p. 109

Chapter two

1. Quote in Gude, p. 19, from Massignon, Daniel 'Le Voyage en Mésopotamie et La Conversion de Louis Massignon en 1908', pp. 148-149. Islamochristiana 14, 1988

2. ibid., p. 19

3. Six. Itinèraire. p.18

4. ibid., p. 21

5. Bazin, pp. 5-7

6. ibid., p. 8. Letter to a friend Feb. 24, 1893

7. ibid., p. 8. Letter to a friend Apr. 17, 1892 and Nov. 8, 1893

8. Six. Itinèraire, p. 27

9. Bazin, p.11

10. ibid., pp.13-15

11. Six. Itinèraire, p.35

12. ibid., p. 36

13. Bazin, p. 19

14. ibid., p. 71

15. Six. Itinèraire, p. 38

16. ibid., p. 42

17. ibid., p.46

18. ibid., p. 52

19. ibid., p. 50

20. ibid., p. 56

21. ibid., p. 56

22. ibid., p. 56

23. ibid., p. 68

24. ibid., p. 54

25. ibid., p. 57

26. ibid., p. 56

27. Charles de Foucauld, 1923, "Ecrits Spirituel", Paris. de Gigord

28. Six. Itinèriare, p. 78. Letter to Duvreyier Oct. 2, 1888

29. Bazin, p. 101

30. Lepetit, p. 27

31. Bazin, p. 125

32. ibid., p.126

33. ibid., p. 126

34. ibid., p. 141

35. Lepetit, p. 30

36. ibid., p. 31

37. ibid., p. 46

38. ibid., p. 47

39. ibid., p. 43

40. ibid., p. 67

41. Inner Search, Letters, p. 141

42. Testimonies, p. 23

43. Destremau/Moncelon, p. 42

44. ibid., p. 45

45. Gude, p. 24

46. Testimonies, p. 21

47. Destremau/Moncelon, p. 48

48. Gude, p. 33

49. ibid., p. 39

50. ibid., p. 41-42 from D. Massignon, Le Voyage p. 146

51. ibid., p. 50

52. Destremau/Moncelon, p. 65

53. Gude, p. 53

54. ibid., p. 67 from Claudel-Massignon, Letter 26, Feb. 19, 1910

55. ibid., p. 72

56. Destremau/Moncelon, p. 111

57. Six. L'Aventure, p. 153

58. ibid., p. 214

59. Parole Donnée, p. 69

60. Testimonies, p. 28. Talk given at Sorbonne, March 18, 1959

61. Parole Donnée, p. 71

62. Opèra Minora, Vol. II, p. 775

63. Six Itineraire, p. 83 from Ecrits Spirituel

64. Parole Donnée, p. 281; Testimonies, p.39; Opèra Minora, Vol ll, p. 831

65. Le Voyage., p. 190

66. Foucauld, Charles de, Ecrits Spirituel, 1923. Paris, de Gigord quoted in Six. Itinéraire, p. 83

67. Le Voyage, p. 192

68. ibid., p. 193, note 149

69. Six. L'Aventure, p. 73

70. Keryell, p. 63

71. L'Herne, p. 115

72. Testimonies, p. 22

73. Jesus Caritas, no. 30, in Inner Search

74. Six. L'Aventure, p. 197

75. Six. Itineraire, p. 373, and L'Aventure, p. 214

76. Six. L'Aventure, p. 210

77. ibid., p. 205

78. "A Time with Charles de Foucauld" (1858-1916). 1998. Paris. Cerf.

Henri de Castries was an explorer who also had a conversion experience to Christianity. It was he who arranged the delivery of Massignon's first letter and thesis on Leo Africanus to the hermit Priest in Tamanrasset.

79. Testimonies, p. 22-23

80. Lepetit, p. 98

81. Opèra Minora, vol.II, p. 780

82. Six. L'Aventure, p. 96

Chapter Three

1. Correspondences p. 126 July 20, 1911. Letter 70

2. Thérèse, 1996, p. 187 Story

3. Gaucher, 1987, p. 22

4. Thérèse, 1996, p. 194 Story

5. ibid., p. 277

6. Gaucher, 1987, p. 147

7. Massignon 1955, p. 59, Diwan

8. ibid., p. 58

9. Thérèse 1977, p. 97 Conversations

10. ibid., p. 138

11. Massignon, 1983, vol. 111, p. 45

12. Isaiah 53:1-3

13. Thérèse, 1977, p. 135 Conversations

14. Thérèse, 1996, p. 200 Poetry

15. Massignon, 1957, p. 126 no. 36 Akhbar

16. Thérèse, 1996, p. 77 Story

17. ibid., p. 276

18. Thérèse 1977. p. 107, Conversations

19. Akhbar, 1957, p. 135 no.50

20. Massignon, 1955, p. 93 m. no. 57 Diwan

21. ibid, p. 48 m. no. 11

22. Thérèse, 1996, p. 165 Story

23. Gaucher, 1982, p. 163

24. Thérèse, 1996, p. 211 Story

25. Massignon, 1955, p. 52, m. no. 15 and 16 Diwan

26. ibid., p. 60, m. no. 23

27. ibid., p. 106, Y no. 1

28. ibid., p. 49, m. no. 12

29. Thérèse, 1996, p. 99-100 Story

30. Six. p. 50

31. Thérèse. 1996.p.214 Story

32. ibid.

33. Clarke, 1997, p. 247

34. ibid., p. 246

35. ibid., 1977, p. 81

36. ibid., p. 205
37. Mason, 1979, p. 75
38. Massignon, 1995, p. 285 abridged
39. Massignon, 1983, vol. 111 p. 35
40. ibid., p. 51
41. Massignon, 1983, Vol. 11 p. 340
42. Mason, 1995, p. 90
43. Massignon, 1994, p. 289 abridged
44. Thérèse, 1996, p. 203 Poems
45. Clarke, 1977, p. 292 Conversations

Chapter Four

1 Englebert, p. 46

2. ibid., p. 12

3. ibid., p. 13

4. Hoeberichts, See chapter 1

5. Franciscan Institute, Muscat, p. 2

6. Englebert p. 16-17

7. Early Documents, p. 187

8. Early Documents "Testament" p. 124 and Englebert p. 32

9. Englebert, p. 33

10. Early Documents p.89, and Englebert, p. 34

11. Matthew 10:7-13

12. Englebert, p. 43

13. Muscat p. 6

14. Englebert, p. 158

15. Early Documents, Jacques de Vitry p. 582

16. Englebert, p. 174

17. Hoeberichts, p. 42

18. ibid., p. 30

19. ibid., p. 42

20. Monograph by Louis Massignon in Opera Minora vol. lll p. 102. Original in a revue of a short political and economic history of Damietta, published in 1949 at the Dom Bosco Institute in Alexandria, edited by the Egyptian Chamber of Commerce in Damietta.

21. Early Documents, p. 231

22. ibid., p. 41 and 45

23. Englebert, p. 201-205 and Documents, p. 45

24. Englebert, p. 219-222

25. Documents, p. 264

26. ibid., "A letter to the Entire Order", p. 118

27. Destremau/Moncelon, p. 245, 246

28. ibid., p. 245

29. Documents, "Letter to the Faithful", p. 46

30. ibid., "Salutation of the Virtues" p. 164

31. Documents, Chapter XIV "Early Rule" p. 73

32. ibid., p. 73

33. Documents, Chapter XVI p, 74

34. Hoeberichts, p. 228 note 55

35. Documents, Chapter XVI p. 74

Chapter Five

1. Keryell, p. 63

2. Encyclopedia Britannica 1997. "Egypt"

3. From a taped interview in Lebanon in August 1972 which Mary Kahil made for Jacques Keryell

4. Keryell, p. 162 (unpublished journal notes, courtesy Daniel Massignon)

5. Keryell, p. 100-101 (from taped interview with Mary Kahil)

6. Keryell, p. 102

7. Mt. 5:44

8. Rom. 5:10

9. Keryell, p. 375

10. Keryell, p. 138.

11. Keryell. p. 268 November 29, 1950 letter from Massignon to Mary Kahil

12. Gude, p. 151

13. Keryell, Letter 73 November 10, 1944

14. Gude, p. 154-155

15. Keryell, p. 355. Note refers to Hallaj, Diwan-Muqatta' a-34

16. Keryell, p. 271. Massignon Letter 168 from Paris May 20, 1951

17. Keryell, p. 129-131

18. Keryell, p. 131

19. Keryell, p. 112-116

20. Keryell. p. 332

21. Keryell. p. 330

22. Keryell. p. 331

23. Keryell. p. 326

24. Keryell. p. 328

25. Massignon, 1983 Parole Donnée, p. 273

26. Quoted in Keryell, p. 129-130. Written January 15, 1953

27. ibid., p. 336

28. ibid., p. 329

29. ibid., p. 334

30. ibid., p. 334

31. ibid., p. 335

32. ibid., p. 338

33. ibid., p. 340

34. From a private collection

Chapter Six

1. Massignon in Opera Minora vol.III p. 627 The Apostolate of Suffering and Reparative Compassion in the 13th Century: The example of Christine the Admirable (1950)

2. Massignon Opera Minora vol. III, p. 635

3. Opera Minora vol.III p. 640

4. Massignon 1989, p. 165-166

5. Gies p. 31

6. Eph. 6:10, 6:17

7. Lk. 2:35

8. Hallaj, Akhbar 36

9. Trask 1996 p. 128

10. Massignon 1962, p. 143-146 [trans. Buck]

11 Examen de l'aspect "théopathique" du témoinage de Jeanne d'Arc In Bulletin des Amis du Vieux-Chinon, no. 6, 1961-1962 pp. 286-294. In Massignon 1994, p. 404

12. Destremau/Moncelon 1994, p. 404

13. Massignon 1987, in Keryell. Letter X Vigil of Christmas 1956, to Badaliya. P. 407

Chapter Seven

1. Opera Minora vol.lll p.716. Massignon's eldest son, Yves, died at the age of 20 on October 29, 1935 of tuberculosis.

2. ibid., p. 722

3. Luke 1:28-56. New American Bible

4. Matthew 1:18-25

5. Luke 2:1-40

6. Matthew 2:1-23

7. Luke 2:41-52

8. John 2:1-12

9. Matthew 12:46-50

10. John 19:26-27

11. Pickthal, Al-e-Imran Sura 3 verse 36

12. ibid., Sura 3 verse 37

13. Yusufali/Picthal, Maryam Sura 19 verse 16-34

14. ibid., Al-Baqara Sura 2 verse 87

15. ibid., Al-Ma'da Sura 5 verse 110

16. Pickthal, An-Nisa' Sura 4 verse 157

17. ibid., Sura 4 verse 158

18. Christmas 1948, letter 148 to Mary Kahil in Keryell p. 257

19. Massignon in Keryell. Letter 148 p. 257

20. Author "Mary and the Virgin Heart" in SUFI Winter 1994-95 p. 5

21. Buck, 1997 The Virgin Heart in the writings of Louis Massignon Conference: "Louis Massignon: The Vocation of a Scholar," Notre Dame U

22. Genesis 18:16-19:4

23. Massignon 1989, p. 12

24. Genesis 21:12-13

25. Buck, SUFI Winter 1994-95 p. 8-10

26. Massignon 1989 p. 15

27. ibid., p.19

28. Massignon in Keryell, letter 156 Jan. 10, 1950 p. 264

29. Letter to the Badaliya No. Xll 1958 in Keryell p. 412

30. Massignon 1989, p. 39

31. Buck, SUFI "Mary and the Virgin Heart: Part Two: The Visitation" Winter 1995-96 p.10

32. Buck 1996 p. 63

33. Massignon 1989 p. 133

34. Massignon 1983 p. 19

35. Buck 1994-95 p. 8

36. Massignon 1983, Vol.lll p. 68

37. Massignon, 1989 p.162

38. Merton 1965 p. 158

39. Buck, 1995-96 p. 8

40. Buck, 1996 p. 79

41. Massignon 1983 Vol.II p. 426

Chapter Eight

1. Encyclopedia Britannica Inc. 1996

2. Koran, Al-Kahf, Sura 18:9-18:26. trans. Pickthal.

3. Massignon 1955 p. 61

4. ibid., p. 62

5. Massignon 1954 Les Sept Dormants D'Éphèse, p. 103-107 (Author's translation)

6. Massignon 1997 "Louis Massignon et ses contemporains", p. 342

7. Massignon 1955 Les Sept Dormants D'Éphèse, p. 102

8. Massignon 1955 p. 103

9. Massignon 1955 p. 74, Commentary by Nûr Kasirqî and Alâ Semnâni

10. Massignon 1987 p. 292 letter 201

11. Keryell 1987. p. 227 letter 92

12. Massignon 1992 p. 7 (La Crypte Dolmen des VII Saints Dormants D'Éphèse)

13. ibid., p. 320

14. Massignon 1955 p. 106-107

15. Massignon 1969 Opéra Minora vol. I p.212

16. Massignon 1987 p. 411 Letter XI

17. Massignon 1987 p. 285

18. Massignon 1987 p. 458

19. Massignon 1987 p. 323

Bibliography

Chapter One

Baldick, R. 1955. *The Life of J.-K. Huysmans.* Oxford:Clarendon Press

Destremau, C. and Moncelon, J. 1994. *Louis Massignon.* Paris, PLON

Gude, M.L. 1996. *Louis Massignon: The Crucible of Compassion.* Notre Dame, IN and London: University of Notre Dame Press

Huysmans, J.-K. 1923 Trans, Hastings, A. *Saint Lydwine of Schiedam.* Rockford IL: Tan Books and Publishers, Inc.

Chapter Two

Bazin, René 1921. *Charles de Foucauld; Explorateur du Maroc; Érmite au Sahara* Paris: Librairie PLON

Destremau, Christian and Moncelon, Jean 1994. *Louis Massignon.* Paris: Librairie PLON

Foucauld, Charles de. 1930 reissued abridged 1981. *Meditations of a Hermit.* London: Burnes & Oates. New York: Orbis Books

_____ 1979. Trans. Lucas, Barbara. *Inner Search; Letters (1889-1916)*. New York: Maryknoll

Gude, Mary Louise 1996. *Louis Massignon; The Crucible of Compassion*. Indiana: University of Notre Dame

Lepetit, Charles. 1983. Trans. Griffiths, John. *Two Dancers in the Desert; The Life of Charles de Foucauld*. New York: Orbis Books

Massignon, Daniel. 1988. *Le Voyage en Mesopotamie et La Conversion de Louis Massignon*. Roma: Islamochristiana vol. 14

Massignon, L. *Textes inédits présentés par Keryell, Jacques*. 1987. *Louis Massignon; L'Hospitalité Sacrée*. Paris: Nouvelle Cité

_____ 1995. *Massignon Sur L'Islam*. Paris: L'Herne

_____ 1983. Intro. Monteill, V.M. (1st ed. 1962 at the death of Louis Massignon) *Parole Donnée*. Paris: Edition du Seuil

_____ 1963. Collected texts presented by Moubaraq, Y. *Opéra Minora*. vol. II, lll Liban: Dar Al-Maaref

_____ 1989. Selected and Introduced by Mason, Herbert. *Testimonies and Reflections; Essays of Louis Massignon*. Indiana: University of Notre Dame

Six, Jean-François. 1958. *Itinéraire Spirituel de Charles de Foucauld*. Paris: Éditions du Seuil

_____ 1993. *L'Aventure de L'Amour de Dieu; 80 lettres inédites de Charles de Foucauld à Louis Massignon*. Paris: Éditions du Seuil

Chapter Three

Gaucher, ocd, G. 1982. *The Story of a Life*. San Francisco, CA: Harper

Mason, H.W. 1995. *Al-Hallaj*. Curzon Press, England

_____ 1979. *The Death of al-Hallaj: A Dramatic Narrative*. Notre Dame, Ind./ London: University of Notre Dame Press

Massignon, L. 1955. *Le Diwân D'Al- Hallâj*. Paris: Librairie Orientaliste. Paul Geuthner

_____ 1957. *Akhbar Al-Hallaj*. Paris: Librairie Philosophique. J. Vrin

_____ 1983. *The Passion of al-Hallaj: Mystic and Martyr*. Translated by H. Mason. Princeton, N.J.: Princeton University Press

_____ 1994. *Hallaj: Mystic and Martyr*. Edited and Translated and Abridged by H. Mason. Princeton, N.J.: Princeton University Press

Malicet, Michel. Collected and annotated by. *Les Grandes Correspondances: Claudel-Massignon (1908-1914)* 1973. Paris: Desclée de Brouwer

Six, Jean-François. 1996. trans. John Bowden *Light of the Night* Indiana: Notre Dame Press

Thérèse of Lisieux 1996. *Story of a Soul*. Translated by J. Clarke, ocd. Washington DC: ICS Publications

_____ 1977 *St. Thérèse of Lisieux: Her Last Conversations* Translated by J. Clarke, ocd. Washington DC: ICS Publications

_____ 1996. *The Poetry of Saint Thérèse of Lisieux.* Translated by Donald Kinney, ocd. Washington, DC: ICS Publications

Note: Translations from the *Diwan* and *Akhbar al-Hallaj* by author. An earlier version of this Chapter appeared in the Autumn 1998 issue of SUFI: A Journal of Sufism

Chapter Four

Bonaventure. 1978. Trans. and Intro. by Ewert Cousins. *Bonaventure.* New York: Paulist Press

Chesterton, G.K. 1924. Reprint 1989. *Saint Francis of Assisi.* New York: Image Books Doubleday

Destremau, Christian and Moncelon, Jean. 1994. *Louis Massignon.* Paris: Librairie PLON

Englebert, Omer. 1965. *St. Francis of Assisi: A Biography.* Ann Arbor, Michigan: Servant Books, Franciscan Herald Press

Francis and Clare: *The Complete Works.* 1982. Trans. and Intro. by R.J. Armstrong, O.F.M., B.C.Ignatius, O.F.M. New York: Paulist Press

Francis of Assisi. 1999. *Early Documents.* Eds. R.J. Armstrong, O.F.M., J.A.W. Hellmann, O.F.M., W.J.Short, O.F.M. St. Bonaventure, N.Y.: Franciscan Institute. New York, London, Manila: New City Press

Gude, Mary Louise. 1996. *Louis Massignon; The Crucible of Compassion.* Indiana: University of Notre Dame

Hoeberichts, J 1997. *Francis and Islam.* Illinois, Quincy: University Franciscan Press

Massignon, Louis. 1963. Collected texts presented by

Moubaraq, Y. *Opéra Minora* vols. II, lll Liban: Dar Al-Maaref

Muscat, ofm, Noel. 1999. *St. Francis of Assisi Malta*. Franciscan Institute from Communications Office, Rome. Internet ofm.org.1/info/Francis1.html

Short, O.F.M. William J. 1999. *Poverty and Joy: The Franciscan Tradition*. Maryknoll: New York, Orbis Books

Chapter Five

Gude, M. L. 1996. *Louis Massignon: The Crucible of Compassion*. Indiana, London: Notre Dame Press

Massignon, L. 1987. Unpublished texts presented by Jacques Keryell. *L'Hospitalité Sacrée* . Paris: Nouvelle Cité

Massignon, L. 1983. *Parole donnée*. Paris: Éditions du Seuil

Note: Translation of French texts by author.

Chapter Six

Collection 1996. *Fresh Verdicts on Joan of Arc.* Edited by B. Wheeler and C. Wood. New York and London: Garland Publishing, Inc

Destremau, Christian and Moncelon, Jean. 1994. *Massignon*. Paris: Librairie PLON

Gies, F. 1981. *Joan of Arc: The Legend and the Reality*. New York: Harper & Row Publishers

Hallaj, 1957. *Akhbar Al-Hallaj*. Edited by L. Massignon and P.Kraus, 3rd ed. Paris

Joan of Arc. 1996. *Joan of Arc: In Her Own Words*. Edited by W.

Trask. New York: B-O-O-K-S & Co. A Turtle Point Imprint

Massignon, L. 1987. Unpublished texts presented by Jacques Keryell. *L'Hospitalité Sacrée.* Paris, Nouvelle Cité

_____ 1969. Articles collected by Youakim Moubarac. *Opéra Minora* vol. lll. Presses Universitaire de France, Paris

_____ 1962. *Parole Donnée* (Jeanne D'Arc et D'Algérie 1956). Introduced by V. Monteil. Paris

_____ 1989. *Testimonies and Reflections: Essays of Louis Massignon.* Selected and Introduced by H. Mason. Indiana: University of Notre Dame Press

Mason, H. 1988. *Memoir of a Friend.* Indiana: University of Notre Dame Press

Chapter Seven

Buck, D. 1996 (summer edition). *The Heart of the Soul* in The Quest, Wheaton, IL.: The Theosophical Society in America.

_____1994-95 (winter edition). *Mary and the Virgin Heart: A Reflection on the Writings of Louis Massignon and Hallaj.* in *SUFI.* London, England: KNP

_____ 1995-96 (winter edition). *Mary and the Virgin Heart: A Reflection on the Writings of Louis Massignon and Hallaj,* Part 2 The Visitation in *SUFI,* London, England: KNP

Petit, J. 1973. *Claudel - Massignon (1908-1914).* In *Les Grandes Correspondences. Collection dirigée par J. Petit.* Desclée De Brouwer

Massignon, L. 1983. Vol.II and III. *The Passion of al-Hallaj:*

Mystic and Martyr. Translated by H. Mason. Princeton, NJ: Princeton University Press

_____ 1989. *Testimonies and Reflections: Essays of Louis Massignon.* Selected and introduced by H. Mason. Notre Dame, Ind.: University of Notre Dame Press

Merton, T. 1968. *Conjectures of a Guilty Bystander*. New York: Doubleday Image Books

The Islamic Computing Centre, Text of the Koran
73 St. Thomas's Road, London N4 2QJ U.K.

Chapter Eight

Massignon L. 1955. *Les Sept Dormants d'Éphèse en Islam et en Chretiente.* Paris: Librairie Orientaliste Paul Geuthner

_____ 1992. Intro. Daniel Massignon. *La Crypte Dolmen Des VII Saints Dormants d'Éphèse.* Extrait des memoires de la Société d'Emulation des Côtes-du-Nord

_____ 1969. Vol I. Ed. Youakim Moubarek. *Opéra Minora.* Press Universitaire de France.

Rozelet, Anne-Marie. 1997.ed. Keryell, J. In *Louis Massignon et ses Contemporains,* Chapter 21 "*Massignon et les pèlerins des Sept Dormants à Vieux Marché*". Paris: Editions Karthala

Profile

Dorothy C. Buck's own spiritual quest led her from many years as a Classical Ballet performer and teacher to Carmelite spirituality. After writing *The Dance of Life* published in 1987 by Paragon House in NYC her interest in spirituality and psychology led to a Ph.D. in Religion and Literature from Boston University. She has an M.A. in Pastoral Counseling from Emmanuel College with further clinical training at the Boston Institute for Psychotherapy. Along with her private practice as a licensed mental health practitioner and Pastoral Counselor in Somerville, MA. she is an active Catholic lay minister at the Paulist Center in Boston. Her articles have appeared in *Dance Magazine, Living Prayer, SUFI, A Journal of Sufism,* and in *The Quest.*